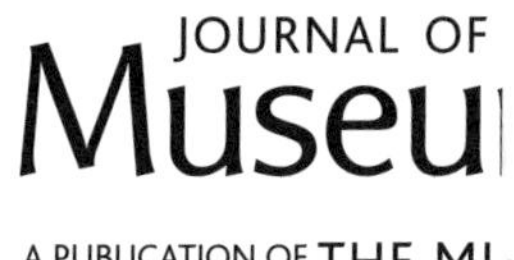

VOLUME 37 • NUMBER 1 • SPRING 2012

Early Learning

A National Conversation

Contents continues on page 2

ISBN 978-1-61132-819-6

ISSN 1059–8650

Cover: Children interact with Yayoi Kusama's *The Obliteration Room* 2002, commissioned for Kids' APT, Queensland Art Gallery | Gallery of Modern Art. Photograph: Natasha Harth

JOURNAL OF
Museum Education
A PUBLICATION OF THE MUSEUM EDUCATION ROUNDTABLE

Early Learning

A National Conversation

The *Museum Education Roundtable* (MER) is a nonprofit organization based in Washington DC, dedicated to enriching and promoting the field of museum education. Through publications, programs, and communication networks, MER fosters professionalism, encourages leadership, scholarship, and research in museum-based learning, and advocates for the inclusion and application of museum-based learning in the general education arena. For more information on MER and its activities, please visit the MER website at www.museumeducation.info and click on 'contact us.' MER members receive the *Journal of Museum Education* as a benefit of membership. To join MER, visit the website at www.museumeducation.info or write to MER at PO Box 15727, Washington, DC 20003.

Journal of Museum Education (ISSN: 1059–8650), is published three times yearly, in the Spring, Summer, and Fall, by Left Coast Press, Inc., in partnership with the Museum Education Roundtable. The journal publishes original papers on theory, training, and practice in the museum education field. Along with articles focused on a specific theme, the journal also features research reports, case studies, tools of the trade, and reviews.

Subscriptions: Members of the Museum Education Roundtable (MER) receive the Journal of Museum Education as a benefit of individual membership. To join MER, visit www.museumeducation.info. Institutional subscriptions should be sent directly to Left Coast Press, Inc. at the address below, addressed to the attention of the Journal Manager. Institutional and non-MER subscriptions may be purchased via check, VISA, MasterCard, or purchase order. All non-institutional subscriptions should be prepaid by personal check, VISA, or MasterCard. Make checks payable to Left Coast Press, Inc. Current prices are listed on the publisher's website, or may be obtained by contacting the publisher at the address below. Payment in U.S. dollars only.

International Orders and Shipping: Add $18.00 per year for postage outside the United States.

Claims: Claims for missing copies will be honored for up to 12 months after date of publication. Missing copies due to losses in transit can be replaced pending availability of reserve stock.

Change of Address: Please notify the publisher six weeks in advance of address changes. Send old address label along with new address to ensure proper identification, and specify name of journal. For individual memberships, MER members should contact MER at membership@museumeducation.info with address changes. For institutional subscriptions, please contact the publisher. ***Postmaster:*** Send all change of address to Left Coast Press, Inc., *Journal of Museum Education,* 1630 N. Main Street, #400, Walnut Creek, CA 94596.

Advertising: Current rates and specifications can be obtained by contacting the Journals Manager, Left Coast Press, Inc., at the address below.

Back issues: Back issues are available through Left Coast Press, Inc., at the address below.

Copyright Permission: For reprint permission requests please contact the publisher, Left Coast Press, Inc., at the address below.

Submission Guidelines: MER welcomes both the submission of original proposals to guest edit sections of the *Journal* and single articles related to theory, training, policy, and practice of museum education. Submission guidelines can be found on the Left Coast Press website (www.lcoastpress.com) and the Museum Education Roundtable website (www.museumeducation.info). Proposals and all manuscripts are subject to peer review by knowledgeable scholars and professional practitioners and, if accepted, may be subject to revision. Materials submitted to the JME should not be under consideration by other publishers, nor should they be previously published in any form. Electronic submissions of issue proposals should include a cover letter, issue abstract, proposed articles and/or authors, and the guest editor's resume. Electronic submissions of single abstracts should include a cover letter, article abstract, and the author's resume. For details on upcoming issue themes, manuscript composition, size, formatting, etc., please consult the Left Coast Press website (www.lcoastpress.com) or the Museum Education Roundtable website (www.museumeducation.info). Reference style should conform to the Chicago Manual of Style, 15th edition. Non-conforming manuscripts will be returned to the author(s) for revision.

Send issue proposals and manuscript correspondence to Tina R. Nolan, Ed.D and Cynthia Robinson, Editors-in-Chief, *Journal of Museum Education,* via email: JMuseEd@gmail.com.

Production and Composition by Detta Penna and Adriane Bosworth

Printed in the United States of America

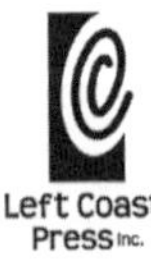

Left Coast Press, Inc.
1630 N. Main Street, #400
Walnut Creek, CA 94596
Phone (925) 935–3380, Fax (925) 935–2916
email journals@lcoastpress.com, web www.lcoastpress.com

Tina R. Nolan and Cynthia Robinson

1973: It was a snowy spring day in Washington D.C. as elementary school teachers sloshed their way to the Renwick Gallery for a workshop called "Food, Fun and Field Trips." A newly formed coalition of museum educators, the Museum Education Roundtable (MER), organized the day's workshop to help teachers create stronger field trips with more direct museum-classroom connections. Together the participants brainstormed pre-visit activities, shared expectations about what makes for engaging field trips, and offered suggestions for how to create the best lessons for students in both museum and school contexts. Documented in the very first issue of MER's periodic newsletter, *Roundtable Reports*, we have a rare snapshot of the everyday lives of museum educators during this period.

The decade of the 1970s was a busy time for this emerging profession: Thanks to federal funding streams that supported an influx of urban renewal projects, thousands of new museums opened their doors and visitation rates were at an all-time high.[1] Museum educators were busy creating the educational tools they needed to serve visitors in new ways:

> New definitions of museum literacy were formed, new frameworks for evaluating programs and exhibits were developed, new guidelines for tours emerged, new ideas on professional development were put forth, new recommendations on how to partner with schools were made, and new organizations such as the Museum Education Roundtable, the Education Committee of AAM, and the Visitor Studies Association were formed.[2]

1984: With a decade of *Roundtable Reports* in hand, Mary Alexander and Ken Yellis (the first editors of *Roundtable Reports*) and Susan Nichols (MER Editorial Committee member) put forth the first anthology of Roundtable Reports articles, *The Museum Education Anthology: Perspectives on Informal Learning, a Decade of Roundtable Reports*.[3] Here we see some of the first collections of

Journal of Museum Education, Volume 37, Number 1, Spring 2012, pp. 5–10.

writings on topics ranging from "adults in museums" to "exhibition reviews," to "volunteers." A year later, *Roundtable Reports* was renamed the *Journal of Museum Education*, and became the first professionally edited and designed journal dedicated to promoting and reporting on theory, training, and practice in the museum education field. Clearly, the profession of museum education had come into its own. As the body of related literature grew, so, too, did the call for a more formalized research agenda:

> In an early issue of the *Journal of Museum Education*, [John] Falk and [Lynn] Dierking (1984) called for museum education to focus its research agenda specifically on *museum learning* as it differentiated itself from *school learning*... [In a separate article, Mary Ellen] Munley urged museum researchers to distinguish the difference between "evaluation," "audience research," and "education research" and develop a conceptual direction for each.[4]

1992: In the second anthology, *Patterns in Practice: Selections from the Journal of Museum Education*,[5] one can witness the field hitting its stride:

> The changes taking place in museum education can be understood within the larger context of an evolving museum environment in which the current trend is toward an expanded public service role. Museum education in recent years has also moved toward greater public service. Formal tours are giving way to informal programs; cognitive learning objectives are being replaced by affective learning; school tours are being joined by programs for families and the adult general public... They also reflect changes in educational theory that incorporate new research and validate multiple learning styles.[6]

2000: At the beginning of the 21st century the museum education profession appeared poised to lead museums to a new future. Joanne Hirsch and Lois Silverman, editors of the third anthology, *Transforming Practice: Selections from the Journal of Museum Education 1992–1999*,[7] urged museum educators to recognize change not only in the profession, but for museums, and for society as a whole:

> Changes in political, social, and economic factors both inside and outside the museum have given rise to compelling strategies and programs. From advocating for diversity to utilizing new technologies,

> from testing educational theories to mounting exhibitions on volatile topics, responses in museum practice over the past 10 years have slowly and subtly transformed the nature of museums and the face of museum education.[8]

Where We're Headed…

2012: Armed with a base of literature and actively involved in organizations such as MER, where opportunities to network and connect practice across institutions abound, many museum educators are well aware of the call for museums to play a stronger role in serving communities. To that end, museum educators are beginning to move out of the proverbial basements of their respective institutions to assume a place in the local and national dialogues about public education, social justice, and community engagement. This issue of the *JME* provides compelling ways to do just that. Marsha Semmel, from the Institute for Museum and Library Services, discusses the blurring of boundaries between learning settings and urges museums to become active players in the out-of-school-time movement.

In some ways, what's old is new again. From 1973 to 1979, *Roundtable Reports* captured the experiences of museum educators through stand-alone articles, exhibition and book reviews, and listings of upcoming events and professional development opportunities. Between 1980 and 2011, each issue of *Roundtable Reports* and the *JME* was guest-edited with a specific focus on single topics that provided in-depth, research-based articles for readers to examine.

Our new format is a blending of the best of both of these approaches. Readers will find each issue has a guest-edited section dedicated to a single topic. In addition, readers will also find a variety of research articles, case studies, perspectives, reviews and tools submitted by authors from both within and without the field of museum education. It is our hope that this new, differentiated format can mirror the best of teaching and learning in this medium.

There is something for every type of learner in each issue: For those who thrive on formal research articles, those who yearn for tools they can use immediately, those who want to understand trends in this sector, those who are politically minded activists, those who are looking for recommendations about the latest books, programs and exhibits to view, and for those who want to examine a single topic from a variety of perspectives, our aim is to provide useful literature for every reader.

The new format and design of the *JME* could not have happened without the support of Jill Overlie, President of MER, and the Museum Education Roundtable Board, its Publications Committee, and the MER members themselves. Special thanks to my friend and colleague, Cynthia Robinson, for her insights and planning with me about the contents of the new format. In this case, two heads are certainly better than one. Thanks, also, to the members of the MER Publications Committee for the tireless creativity they lent to determining new look of the *JME*: Karen Daly, Carol Krucoff, Elisabeth Nevins, Tina Nolan, Jill Overlie, Victoria Ramirez, Nancy Richner, Cynthia Robinson, Laureen Trainer, and our fearless leader and Publications Committee Chair, Beth Maloney. We also extend a special thanks to Eric Mongeon, of Mongeon Projects, Inc. who donated his graphic design expertise to guide us in our work. We are so pleased to be partnered with our publisher, Left Coast Press, and their fine staff for supporting our new direction: Mitch Allen, Bridget Moar, and Stefania Van Dyke. An extra special thanks to Detta Penna, graphic designer for Left Coast Press, and good friend to the *JME*, for taking our vision and making it a beautiful reality.

Museum educators are the driving force behind the content of the *JME*, and to that end we hope you will consider writing for a future issue. Guidelines for single manuscript submissions and guest editor proposals can be found on both the Left Coast press website at www.lcoastpress.com and the Museum Education Roundtable website at www.museumeducation.info. Single articles and guest editor proposals are accepted on an ongoing basis.

We welcome your submissions and look forward to expanding the conversation and contributions to the museum education literature through the new *JME* format. Should you need to speak with either me or Cynthia, please email us directly at: Tina.Nolan@nl.edu and Cynthia.Robinson@tufts.edu. You can also send a message to both of us at our JME gmail account: JMuseEd@gmail.com.

Tina Nolan

Notes

1. Marjorie Schwartzer, *Riches, Rivals & Radicals: 100 Years of Museums in America*, (Washington DC, American Association of Museums, 2006), 22.
2. Tina R. Nolan, *The Leadership Practice of Museum Educators* (unpublished doctoral dissertation), National Louis University, Chicago, IL, 2010, p.28. This dissertation will be available on ProQuest in 2012.
3. Susan K. Nicols, Ken Yellis, & Mary Alexander, *The Museum Education Anthology: Perspectives on Informal Learning, a Decade of Roundtable Reports*, (Washington DC, Museum Education Roundtable, 1984).

4. Tina R. Nolan, *The Leadership Practice of Museum Educators.*
5. Museum Education Roundtable, *Patterns in Practice.*
6. Ibid., 10.
7. Joanne S. Hirsch & Lois H. Silverman, Eds., *Transforming Practice: Selections from the Journal of Museum Education 1992–1999* (Washington DC, 2000).
8. Ibid., introduction.

About the Authors

Tina R. Nolan, Ed.D, Co-Editor of the *JME*, is Associate Director of Partnerships in the National College of Education at National Louis University. In addition, Dr. Nolan works with museums and other not-for-profit educational organizations as an independent education consultant, researcher, guest lecturer, and writer.

Cynthia Robinson, Co-Editor of the *JME*, is the director of museum studies at Tufts University. She spent 25 years working in and with museums and has extensive experience in developing programs, curricula, and exhibitions, as well as in museum management and administration.

Early Learning

A National Conversation

Sharon Shaffer

At a time when early learning is receiving national attention, we are also hearing reports of near-record low confidence in U.S. public schools.[1] So what does that mean for museums? As a society we have a responsibility to ensure that our youngest children are engaged in quality learning experiences; and museums, as important community institutions, will need to seek opportunities and contribute in new ways to this critical effort, on a local level at the very least and nationally where possible.

Armed with research about the significance of the early years and the increasing attention to early learning, educators are beginning to think seriously about strategic efforts toward developing enriched and educative experiences for our young children.[2] As members of the museum community, we have an important role to play in shaping the learning of this young generation, joining forces with educators and policy makers from across the community to meet early learning goals.

Within museums we need to assess the current state of affairs related to early learning, review the research and identify gaps, explore current practices noting strengths and weaknesses, share new ideas, and create a network of individuals dedicated to supporting the expanding audience of young children in museums. There is much work to be done, but there is evidence that early learning is valued and support is growing, leading to increased opportunities for children that broaden horizons, introduce new ideas, develop age-appropriate skills, and engage children's imagination and sense of wonder.

A recent commitment by the Smithsonian Institution recognizes the value of early learning through financial support of a planning grant that will bring together experts in early childhood education and researchers focused on museums

Journal of Museum Education, Volume 37, Number 1, Spring 2012, pp. 11–16.

and young children. Collectively this national advisory committee will answer key questions about what we know about this audience through research and practice, where the gaps are in our knowledge, and what we want to know. This information will be critical in planning the National Symposium on Early Learning in Museums and sets the stage for discussion and strategic thinking related to research. Plans also include establishing a national network of museum professionals with an interest in and passion for serving young children in museums. Ultimately, a publication dedicated to young children in museums is a planned outcome of the symposium to establish a future path for research, theory, and practice for serving our youngest museum goers.

The education of our children is a community affair, with efforts coming from traditional institutions such as schools as well as more informal community-based programs in museums, libraries, and other cultural institutions. To effectively educate our nation's children, it will be important for us to work collaboratively within the community, but also within our inner circle of museum professionals. In the Fall 2010 *Journal of Museum Education,* Cynthia Robinson wrote of the need for museum educators to become involved in broader issues within their institutions. She suggested that success is linked to "collectivity," where educators work together and join in "collective discussions and actions, and a willingness to leave one's comfort zones to become involved in critical issues that affect museum education."[3] As our profession addresses this burgeoning audience of young children, our success will be tied to our ability to come together to understand the developmental capacity and learning style of this audience in the context of museum spaces while also creating a vision that includes design of exhibits and a focus on families and programs for younger visitors.

This issue, *Early Learning: A National Conversation,* offers a platform for discussion about young children in museums and will hopefully serve as a catalyst for the development of early learning programs of excellence in museums. In "Trends in Museums," Marsha Semmel, the Institute of Museum and Library Services (IMLS) Director of Strategic Partnerships, defines the framework and opportunities present in today's world. She makes a case that early learning is the foundation for life-long learning and that this national conversation is taking place "… amid a broader context shaped by new research findings, thoughtful and strategic investment of ever scarcer funds, priorities around more alignment across different learning domains, the digital technologies, and the recognition of interconnections between formal and informal learning settings." Semmel encourages museums to overcome challenges and seize opportunities to participate in the conversation.

Researchers Barbara Wolf and Elee Wood from The Children's Museum of Indianapolis ground the issue with current research taking place primarily in children's museums, but describe lessons learned that apply to almost any museum experience. Their focus is on scaffolding learning through purposeful interactions between adult and child, a strategy that "... can inform adults and simultaneously help children stretch to new levels of understanding and achievement." The message is clear that possibilities for expanding learning exist with collaboration from curators, educators, and exhibit developers.

Research in children's museums informs our thinking and provides lessons that at times extend to the more traditional museum setting where exhibitions are not designed with the active learning style of young children in mind. But what is really happening in art, history, culture, and science museums when it comes to early learners? Without a national network currently in place, nor comprehensive data available outlining museum programs for early learners, Betsy Bowers approached the need to capture the moment in early learning programming through an informal on-line survey. The results, although interesting, are just the first step in understanding early learning practices in cultural institutions. The data suggests that while educators recognize the significance of early learning in museums there is a need to bring our collective knowledge to bear on future practice. The survey further indicates that the interest in early learning warrants "... a larger and more thorough evaluation of early childhood programming in museums."

Early learning research and practice is not new to the community outside of museums, having gained a sense of primacy since the introduction of Head Start in President Johnson's War on Poverty. Understanding gleaned from years of early childhood research and practice offers tremendous potential to inform practices and provide insights for those working within the museum profession. Authors Pamela Krakowski, Rochelle Ibanez Wolberg, Allison Goff, and Melina Mallos look at the intersection of early childhood research, theory, and practice with potential programming within museum settings. Krakowski examines the role of play in learning and applies it to the world of museums in "Museum Superheroes: The Role of Play in Young Children's Lives" describing how young children connect to the art of Andy Warhol through imaginative play. For children it is the opportunity to explore what is important in their lives and make connections to the world that is ripe for learning regardless of place. Wolberg and Goff discuss thinking routines developed by researchers from Harvard's Project Zero and suggest that these strategies are effective methods of creating meaning and making thinking visible in both formal and informal learning environments. The authors posit that students benefit when teaching techniques cross boundaries between classrooms and museums. Mallos offers an international example of early childhood practice in an art museum setting. In a museum that embraces young audiences and contemporary art, there is a collaborative effort that brings together curators, artists, and children. The process begins with research that defines best practice for engaging young audiences in museums and includes collaborative planning that contributes to the design of gallery exhibits. The illustrations in all three articles bridge the world of young children and early learning with the galleries in museums, highlighting the potential for success.

Museums are more than repositories for objects, art, and natural specimens. They are uniquely positioned to unite community members during times of crisis or even in everyday experiences. Case studies of two museums illustrate the potential for building community relationships and the impact of an institution's actions. Kate Barron describes a museum's response to crisis following Hurricane Katrina in New Orleans. The Ogden Museum of Southern Art sought out schools in the aftermath of the storm as a step to rebuilding a community and the lives of its citizens. Hers is a story of collaboration with neighborhood schools, bringing methods to the classroom and the museum that engage young children in exploring their world and understanding a sense of place. Allison Wickens offers a different story of community, one that emphasizes the value of being responsive to neighboring schools and community members to ensure that museum visits are relevant for young audiences. Wickens raises the question of mission in her article and suggests that there may be a time and place to reconsider, although carefully, the mission of the education department with an open-mind toward revision.

Each of these authors shares a story about early learning in museums, a message that we hope will serve as a catalyst for a new generation of meaningful and relevant programs for our nation's youngest museum-goers. As members of the museum profession we can make a difference.

Museums have the potential to make a significant contribution to the education of America's children, but will need to gather information through research and practice from colleagues in museums as well as from early childhood practitioners and researchers outside of the museum world. This is an opportune moment for making a difference in the lives of children, one that we should all recognize and set as a serious priority.

Notes

1. www.gallup.com/poll/148724/Near-Record-Low-Confidence-Public-Schools.aspx
2. Martin S. Dworkin, *Dewey on Education*, New York: Teachers College Press, 1959.
3. Cynthia Robinson and Tina R. Nolan, "Mission, Money, and Authority, Part II." *Journal of Museum Education*, 33.3 (Fall 2010), 214.

About the Author

Sharon Shaffer, PhD, is the Founding Director for the Smithsonian Early Enrichment Center (SEEC), the Smithsonian Institution's model museum-based program for young children. She leads the lab school at the Smithsonian and consults with schools and museums nationally and internationally designing educational programs and applying museum-based methodology to learning experiences for students Pre-K–12. Dr. Shaffer is a graduate instructor for the Curry School of Education at the University of Virginia where she teaches Social Foundations of American Education.

An Opportune Moment

Museums in the National Conversation on Early Learning

Marsha L. Semmel

Abstract The national conversation on early learning and its importance as a foundation of lifelong learning has reached a tipping point, with increased attention at the local, state, and federal level. The context for this conversation includes a growing corpus of respected research on early childhood development that points to a critical learning "pivot point" by age eight and an understanding that learning opportunities need to include the "whole child," encompassing cognitive, emotional, physical, and social dimensions. Current early learning policy and funding priorities emphasize a coordinated and strategic investment of resources, research- and evidenced-based practice, and an alignment across different institutional learning domains in order to achieve system-wide outcomes. Museums have the opportunity to build on their knowledge and experience to contribute meaningfully to this national effort. The author discusses several national, public/private efforts—including increased recognition of a cradle-to-grave learning "ecosystem"—that are informing the early learning conversation. How can museums be effective and recognized players in today's learning environment, and what are some challenges and opportunities specifically linked to early learning?

In this article, which explores national trends and programs that reflect a transformed understanding of the interconnections between formal and informal learning, I make three principal points:

1. There is increased national attention to the power of learning in out-of-school environments, including museums. Recent research on learning and the rapid deployment of new technologies are two key drivers of this recognition.

Journal of Museum Education, Volume 37, Number 1, Spring 2012, pp. 17–28.

2. There is a concomitant and widespread acknowledgement of the significance of the early childhood years as definitive for future academic, social, and economic success.
3. Museums have enormous opportunities to play a more central role in this redefined learning landscape. Success, however, will depend on a number of factors, including using the community (not the institution) as the frame of reference. The potential for museums to gain greater recognition (and, hopefully, resources) in their role as centers for learning is yet to be recognized by civic officials, policy makers, and funders.

The Learning Revolution: Defining a Learning Ecosystem

John Falk and Lynn Dierking pioneered my understanding of museums and "free choice" learning. They drove home the fact that significant learning time, the *majority* of potential "free choice learning" time, even for school-aged youth, occurs outside the classroom. In such books as *Lessons Without Limits: How free-choice learning is Transforming Education,* Falk and Dierking promoted awareness and respect for the knowledge, experiences, passions, and abilities that learners of all ages bring to a museum and encouraged us to find ways to meet these learners' needs. With other researchers and practitioners, they positioned the museum as one of many learning sites within a larger community learning landscape.[1]

This recognition of the scope and impact of out-of-school learning is growing. Increased numbers of education leaders, funders, and policy makers are promoting a holistic vision of learning that (1) places learners at the center, (2) sees learning as a year-long, 24/7 enterprise, (3) recognizes that learners of all ages are increasingly taking charge of their learning and seeing themselves as "free agents" in an increasingly de-institutionalized learning environment, and (4) understands the power of rapidly deploying digital technologies to de-materialize the boundaries between home, school, museum, library, park, and other learning places, and link geographically disparate learners through online communities of interest.

Scholars Douglas Thomas and John Seely Brown write of "a new culture of learning" where "play, questioning, and — perhaps most important — imagination lie at the very heart of arc-of-life learning." According to Thomas and Brown, the most effective learning in "our world of constant change" builds bridges between today's "massive information network that provides almost unlimited access and resources to learn about anything" and personalized and structured environments that allow for "unlimited agency to build and experiment."[2]

These (and many other) efforts at re-visioning learning are fueled by the rapid proliferation of digital technologies that enable increased personalization and customization of learning experiences. They are supported by other factors, including increased research about the brain and the cognitive, social, and emotional dimensions of learning; new knowledge about youth development; studies on the qualities of effective learning in both in- and out-of-school settings; and the belief that today's learners (and tomorrow's workers) need proficiency in skills as well as content in order to have the capacity to address the challenges of the global knowledge society. While these developments have inspired vigorous debates about the need for new curricula and skills, changes in the role of teachers and administrators, and redefinitions of assessment and performance (as well as the importance of out-of-school and after-school learning) most museums, with few exceptions, remain outside these conversations. Rarely are museums recognized as organizations well equipped to play a more significant and relevant role in promoting effective learning.

A community-wide, lifelong approach to learning informs *Learning 2025, A Working Paper from a Grantmaker Convening* (September 30–October 1, 2010) of Grantmakers for Education, a membership organization of more than 280 private and public philanthropies that support "improved education outcomes for students from early childhood through higher education." *Learning 2025* envisions a vibrant "learning ecosystem" in which "the boundary between 'school' and 'community' has blurred." In order to foster "personalized learning in a community context," the many learning environments within communities need to provide "rich opportunities [for learners] to apply their knowledge in context" and "benefit from cross-sector support systems that address both academics and non-academics."[3]

Youth and their parents increasingly share this view of "unbounded" learning. Since 2003, more than 2.2 million students, parents, teachers, librarians, principals, technology leaders and district administrators have participated in the annual poll conducted by the *Speak Up* National Research Project on the role of technology in learning. The 2010 survey findings, presented in two reports, *The New 3 E's of Education: Enabled, Engaged, Empowered*, show that students, and increasingly parents, want learning environments that are "socially-based, un-tethered, and digitally rich," with students, as "free agent learners," seeking out learning resources on their own, "following a passion for a topic or subject not fully explored through their coursework or to self-remediate when they feel they need additional help or support."[4] *Transforming American Education: Learning Powered by Technology: the National Education Technology Plan* emphasizes the potential of technology to create a seamless, "always on" education and learning infrastructure that moves us to a "learning model that brings together teaching teams and students in classrooms, labs, libraries, museums, workplaces, and homes — anywhere in the world where people have access devices and adequate Internet connections." While museums are mentioned in the plan, they are not a focus.[5]

One publication that does focus on museums, especially science museums, is the National Research Council's 2009 *Learning Science in Informal Environments: People, Places, and Communities*, a landmark study describing an "ecological framework" for learning that highlights 'the cognitive, social and, cultural learning processes and outcomes that are shaped by distinctive features of particular settings, learner motivations and backgrounds and associated learning expectations." This framework encompasses different disciplinary approaches and takes into account "the compound set of influences on learning and development originating from a person's experiences across myriad institutional contexts and social niches..." The study synthesizes what we know (and how much we *don't* know) about the impact of museums on out-of-school science learning.[6]

Why are museums so infrequently recognized as vibrant, 21st-century learning venues when there are many documented examples of their providing memorable learning experiences for people of all ages, when they continue to be considered trusted institutions, and when they occupy a potentially powerful community position as family-friendly places promoting intergenerational learning? One reason is that museums remain part of the generally devalued "informal" learning sector. Another is a nagging public perception of museums as elitist and often inaccessible learning institutions, a perception that is unfortunately true in many instances. Other reasons include the lack of collective research and evidence on the impact of museum learning experiences and the relatively siloed sharing of what data exist. We still lack comprehensive data on the U.S. museum sector as a whole, let alone compelling statements of the field's educational impact. Much evaluation still occurs at the level of the individual museum program, exhibition, or institution, making it impossible to "scale up" research results.

Despite the deep historical connections between museums and schools (and seminal works like AAM's *Education and Equity: Education and the Public Di-*

mension of Museums), many policy makers and funders still harbor fairly traditional notions of museum educational programs, and many programs don't dispute these assumptions. Moreover, despite examples of exciting partnerships with other educational organizations, museums still tend to operate (even within the same community) as "islands," unconnected in significant programmatic ways to each other or to other learning venues or providers. There are few robust, well established, community-based, museum learning networks or systems. Finally, as in many domains, museum professionals tend to talk with each other, using field-specific language, benchmarks, and practice. They remain unfamiliar with other learning research and pedagogy, and their non-museum peers are similarly uninformed of current museum practice.

In a recent effort to address the absence of museums (and libraries) from these national discussions, IMLS worked with a national task force of museum and library leaders on *Museums, Libraries and 21st Century Skills*. The report situates evolving practice in museums and libraries within this changing world of learning and its policy and strategic implications. It charts the 21st-century museum/library shift, and provides several case studies, a community learning scan, and a self-assessment tool that can help an individual organization position itself along a continuum to achieve its 21st century potential. Building on the long history of museums and libraries and their rich and authentic content, dedicated and knowledgeable staff, and safe and trusted settings for individuals and families, the report notes that all museums and libraries "stand to benefit from becoming more intentional and purposeful about accommodating the lifelong learning needs of people in the 21st century, and doing this work collaboratively in alignment with community needs." The project has led to increased cross-learning-sector discussion, planning, and practice. It has also spawned a formal partnership with the John D. and Catherine T. MacArthur Foundation's digital media and learning initiative. IMLS and MacArthur are co-investing in a series of "learning labs" for teens in museums and libraries around the country.[7]

Implications for Early Learning

The increased recognition of a broader learning ecosystem has implications for early learning practitioners, especially as research and data confirm the learning capacity of the youngest children, privilege a community-wide learning context, and note the increased penetration of new technologies at lower and lower age groups.

The National Research Council's *Taking Science to School: Learning and Teaching Science in Grades K–8* devotes an entire chapter to the "surprisingly sophisticated" science learning and "substantial knowledge" of the natural world that the youngest children master before entering elementary school.[8] In *The 21st Century Learner: The Continuum Begins with Early Learning,* Dr. Alison Gopnik notes that recent scientific research indicates that "an incredible amount of early learning is underpinned by an equally incredible amount of early brain change and brain development" in the youngest of children.[9] Economist James J. Heckman has noted that "The best evidence suggests that learning begets learning. Early investments in learning are effective. ... Learning is a dynamic process and is most effective when it begins at a young age and continues through adulthood."[10] Numerous other studies have concluded that investing in early learning yields substantial economic benefits that are reflected in cost savings in the formal school system, tax revenues, health and welfare systems and the criminal justice system.[11]

The Joan Ganz Cooney Center at Sesame Workshop, with a mission to "foster innovation in children's learning through digital media," has published a number of recent studies on the impact of digital media on young children. *Pockets of Potential: Using Mobile Technologies to Promote Children's Learning* explores recent handheld learning products and research showing how mobile devices may help re-imagine teaching and learning for young children. *Game Changer: Investing in Digital Play to Advance Children's Learning and Health* surveys the educational potential of children's games. *Families Matter: Designing Media for a Digital Age* presents research on how families consider and evaluate digital media products for their young children as well as provide case studies of whole family interactions around digital media.[12] *Zero to Eight: Children's Media Use in America,* an October 2011 research study by Common Sense Media, presents a compelling and current portrait of the digital media use among the youngest (2–4 years) children.[13]

Although there has been federal support for early learning efforts for decades, this issue is receiving heightened attention. President Obama has said, "Learning begins at birth," and in 2009 established an Interagency Policy Board, chaired by Health and Human Services Secretary Kathleen Sibelius. The board's focus on pre-natal through age 8 underscores the importance of health *and* education, the need for family engagement, the need for developing benchmarks and evidence of quality programs and effective practice, a focused research agenda, and a coordinated and integrated system (based on evidence and data) for early learning support that includes school, home, and community.

Accordingly, in addition to longstanding programs like Head Start, Even Start, and 21st Century Community Learning Centers, several new initiatives have made early learning a funding priority. These include such big-ticket Department of Education programs as Race to the Top (which provides financial incentive for state- and system-wide reform and innovation), Invest in Innovation (i3) competitive grants that expand the "implementation of, and investment in, innovative and evidence-based practices, programs and strategies that significantly improve student achievement and close achievement gaps", and Promise Neighborhoods, which support projects that "significantly improve the educational and developmental outcomes of children and youth in our most distressed communities" in order to "transform those communities by providing a cradle-to-career continuum of ambitious, rigorous, and comprehensive education reforms, effective community services, and strong systems of family and community support — with high-quality schools at the center." The first awards in each of these programs included substantial moneys for early learning programs.[14]

In May 2011, the Department of Education and the Department of Health and Human Services announced a new program, a $500 million Race to the Top — Early Learning Challenge Program (RTT-ELC). The goal is to help highly committed states provide more children from birth to age five from low-income families with access to high-quality early learning and development programs. The focus will be support for "breakthrough work that dramatically improves the quality of early learning and development programs serving high-need children." Priority will be "aligning early childhood resources and systems and improving early learning and development standards and assessment, program standards, tiered rating and improvement systems, and early childhood educators."[15] While museums are not the focus of any of these federal efforts, some are participating as part of larger collaborations.

Many states are already on board. In October, 2010, the National Governors Association published "Building Ready States: A Governor's Guide to Supporting a Comprehensive, High-Quality Early Childhood State System." The report asserts: "Public investments in high-quality early childhood programs generate cost savings of between seven percent and 10 percent in other public programs such as economic support and incarceration programs." It suggests six actions that state leaders can take: (1) coordinate early childhood governance though a state early childhood advisory council; (2) build an integrated professional development system; (3) implement a quality rating and improvement system that measures program quality using common metrics; (4) develop a longitudinal and coordinated early childhood data system; (5) align comprehensive early learning guidelines and standards for children from birth to 8 with K–3 content standards; (6) integrate federal, state, and private funding. Accordingly, efforts are proceeding in a number of states.[16]

A coordinated effort by the private sector was launched In February 2011, when the Annie E. Casey Foundation announced The Campaign for Grade-Level Reading, a national ten-year effort that is bringing together more than eighty private funders. The campaign links the low U.S. high school graduation rate to the fact that a large number of children have not achieved reading proficiency before leaving third grade, "the point when educators expect children to pivot from just 'learning to read' to 'reading to learn.'" "Falling short of this critical milestone," according to the campaign, "has continuing and significant consequences for future success in school, work, and life." The campaign seeks to support efforts that make a significant and demonstrable positive impact on the "school readiness challenge," the "chronic absence challenge," and the "summer learning loss challenge." A plethora of private and public organizations have signed on, although museum representation is currently scarce. As of this writing, the campaign is getting off the ground, with plans formulated for national recognition through the 2012 All-America City Award and collaborative efforts at the community level.[17]

IMLS Support for Early Learning: Two Projects and a National Initiative

The Institute of Museum and Library Services has a strong and consistent record of supporting projects in all types of museums and libraries that address the needs of young children and their families. These include the *Countdown to Kindergarten* school readiness program pioneered by the Boston Children's Museum and anchored by museums in other communities around the country; *Good to Grow,* a national initiative of the Association of Children's Museums to "improve the health and wellness of our nation's families through museum programs, exhibits, partnerships, and institutional practices; a multi-institutional research project on "Family Learning in Interactive Galleries" involving the Frist Center for the Visual Arts, the High Museum of Art, and the J.B. Speed Museum of Art; a collaboration involving the Chicago Zoological Society, the Association of Zoos and Aquariums, the Natural Learning Initiative at North Carolina State University, and Chicago Wilderness to develop a corps of early childhood nature play professionals across the country; and projects in other science centers, art museums, history museums, tribal museums and cultural centers.

Two current projects of particular interest are The National Early Childhood Obesity Prevention Pilot Program launched by the Children's Museum of Manhattan, and FLIP (Family Literacy Involvement Program), a collaboration between the Children's Museum of Houston, the Houston Public Library, and the Children's Learning Institute of the University of Texas Health Science Center.

The CMOM project focuses on the community-wide role of museums in the fight against childhood obesity through the customizing of the National Institute of Health's *We Can!* curriculum for children under age eight and their parents. The project has adapted the NIH rubric into a new *Eat Sleep Play* curriculum, created a new permanent exhibition, produced five research reports on the impact of the curriculum on families in low-income communities in the Bronx and New Orleans, is creating a Head Start Wellness policy in collaboration with the United Way of New York City and the Administration for Children's Services and will replicate early health and literacy exhibits and programs inside public housing in East Harlem.

Based on a successful 4-year pilot, the FLIP project is a community-wide program for increasing family literacy, with a focus on newcomer and lower income families. FLIP has created a set of 201 Family Literacy (FLIP) kits that have been duplicated into 2,040 kits and launched for circulation through 35 branches of the Houston Public Library system, including the branch library at the museum itself. The kits are available in four languages, including English, Spanish, Vietnamese, and Chinese. Parents use them at home with their children. Once FLIP was established in Houston, the museum created a national training program for 10 museum/library partners, a web site (www.flipkits.org), and a toolkit for implementation by other communities. The University of Texas's Children's Learning Institute conducted a quasi-experimental controlled comparison study to assess the impact of the kits on parent and child home literacy practices, attitudes, and children's literacy-related skills and attitudes. Study participants who used the FLIP Kits had statistically significant 20 percentage point and above gains in two key areas: (1) parent discovery of the skills and interests of their children and (2) parent intention to incorporate new home reading practices.

In May 2011, IMLS worked with Association of Children's Museums, the American Public Gardens Association, the American Association of Museums, and the Office of the First Lady and the Domestic Policy Council, to launch *Let's Move Museums and Gardens*, part of Mrs. Michele Obama's national campaign against childhood obesity. Museums can register on the IMLS web site and commit to an "overarching" participation goal aimed at enlisting at least 2,000 museums and gardens. Museums must pledge engagement in at least two of four areas: (1) offering interactive experiences that promote healthy eating and physical activity; (2) afterschool, summer, and school-based programs including healthy food choices and physical activity; (3) food options that reflect healthy choices; and (4) food service that incorporates interpretation about healthy food choices.[18]

Each of these projects reflects a system-wide and collaborative approach. In addition, each is rooted in current health and learning research; focuses on the "whole child," parent, and caregiver; demonstrates a serious investment in high quality evaluation and ongoing course correction and a commitment to effective scalability; and promotes broader community and national early learning goals and results. In today's early learning environment, these characteristics will be essential to museums gaining more visibility as "core players" in successful early learning efforts and making meaningful and lasting contributions to addressing this country's serious early learning challenges.

The Early Learning Opportunity for Museums: Five Suggestions

How can museums leverage their expertise, their programs, their sites, and their pedagogical knowledge to become more visible and more "essential" to this societal revolution in learning, especially in the area of early learning?

1. **Look inward**. Assess your organization's strengths and resources for creating effective early learning experiences. What do you bring to the table? How do your museum's vision, mission, and strategic plan support early learning? Think holistically across your entire institution.

2. **Look outward** to ascertain your community's early learning needs and map the ways that different organizations are currently addressing these needs. Where are the gaps? What does your museum have to offer that can help meet the early learning challenges of your community? This "looking outward" should include conversations with individuals (parents, families, other community members) as well as with people in other institutions.

3. **Join forces** with other museums, libraries, social service organizations, and civic entities in strategic collaborations that can improve the quality and effectiveness of learning opportunities for all, especially underserved children and their families.

4. **Define your outcomes** in a broader community context that goes beyond your museum and develop an evaluation plan that links your institution-

specific efforts to broader community goals. Build some "course correction" into your projects, anticipating the unexpected. As metrics of impact are being devised throughout the early learning sector, align your data collection with those metrics.

5. **Take a seat** "at the table" when your community's civic, corporate, philanthropic, and formal educational institutions are formulating policy and addressing learning challenges affecting populations of all ages. Know what and how your museum can make an effective contribution to broader community goals.

We are in an enormously rich and transformational moment where we must all envision (and re-vision) a powerful future for learning, including learning for our youngest learners. Museums have much to offer. It's time to seize the day.

Notes

1. J. H. Falk and Lynn Dierking, "Optimizing out-of-school time: the role of free-choice learning," *New Directions for Youth Development* 97 (Spring 2003): 75–88. IMLS also has a long history of initiatives and publications that situate museum and library learning in a broader context, including *True Needs, True Partners: Museums and Schools Transforming Education* (1996, 2002), *The 21st Century Learner* (2001), *Charting the Landscape, Mapping New Paths: Museums, Libraries and K–12 Learning* (2004), *Nine to Nineteen: Youth in Museums and Libraries, A Practitioner's Guide* (2008), and *Partnership for a Nation of Learners: Joining Forces, Creating Value* (2009). http://www.imls.gov/resources/publications.aspx
2. Douglas Thomas and John Seely Brown, *A New Culture of Learning: Cultivating the Imagination for a World of Constant Change* (2011), 18–19.
3. Grantmakers for Education, "Learning 2025: A Working Paper from a Grantmaker Convening, September 30–October 1, 2010, http://edfunders.org/downloads/GFEreports/GFE_Learning2025.pdf (accessed October 2011).
4. Project Tomorrow Speak Up, *The New 3E's of Education: Enabled, Engaged, Empowered, Speak Up 2010 National Findings, K–12 Students & Parents* (Irvine, CA: Project Tomorrow, 2011), 1–3. Another study, *Year-Round Learning: Linking School, Afterschool, and Summer Learning to Support Student Success,* published in June 2011 by the Harvard Family Research Project, describes year-round learning as "intentional, community-based efforts to connect school, afterschool, and summer learning," and cites "emerging research" as suggesting "that connecting learning environments can lead to better outcomes."
5. U.S. Department of Education, T*ransforming American Education: Learning Powered by Technology: the National Education Technology Plan,* prepared by the Office of Education Technology, (Washington, D.C., 2010): xiii.
6. National Research Council of the National Academies, *Learning Science in Informal Environments: People, Places, and Pursuits,* ed. Philip Bell et al. (Washington, DC: The National Academies Press, 2009).
7. Institute of Museum and Library Services, *Museums, Libraries and 21st Century Skills,* produced by the Office of Strategic Partnerships under the leadership of Marsha Semmel (Washington, DC: 2009), 7.
8. National Research Council of the National Academies, *Taking Science to School: Learning and Teaching Science in Grades K–8,* ed. Richard A. Duschl, Heidi A. Schweingruber, and Andrew W. Shouse (Washington, DC: The National Academies Press, 2007), 53.

9. Alison Gopnik, "The 21st Century Learner: The Continuum Begins with Early Learning" (Keynote address, The 21st Century Learner Symposium, Washington, D.C., September 18 and 19, 2003).
10. James J. Heckman, "Policies to Foster Human Capital" (Paper presented at the Aaron Wildavsky Forum, Richard and Rhoda Goldman School of Public Policy, University of California at Berkeley, February 2000).
11. Belfield, Clive R, *Investing in Early Childhood Education in Ohio: An Economic Appraisal* (New York: Teachers College, Columbia University, 2004). The 2009 *Final Evaluation Report: Lessons Learned from the MELF Community Grants*, produced by the CEED Evaluation Team in Minnesota also offers interesting state-specific findings regarding the impacts of Minnesota Early Learning Foundation's grants to communities to boost early learning opportunities.
12. The Joan Ganz Cooney Center at Sesame Workshop, "Reports," Research and Initiatives, http://www.joanganzcooneycenter.org/Reports.html (accessed October 25, 2011). The *2010 Kids and Family Reading Report*, a national survey released by Scholastic, Inc. in September 2010, offers additional interesting findings on current reading practices of children and their parents, including insights about digital devices and e-books. (http://mediaroom.scholastic.com/themes/bare_bones/2010_KFRR.pdf) A 2005–2010 Department of Education Ready to Learn grant to the Corporation for Public Broadcasting and the Public Broadcasting Service supported several rigorous research and evaluation on the impact of television and digital media on early learners, especially in economically disadvantaged areas. (http://www.cpb.org/rtl/FindingsFromReadyToLearn2005–2010.pdf)
13. Common Sense Media, *Zero to Eight: Children's Media Use in America* (San Francisco: Common Sense Media, Inc, 2011).
14. U.S. Department of Education, "Early Learning Initiative," http://www.ed.gov/early-learning (accessed October 2011).
15. U.S. Department of Education, "Race to the Top — Early Learning Challenge," http://www2.ed.gov/programs/racetothetop-earlylearningchallenge/index.html (accessed October 2011).
16. Rachel Demma, "Building Ready States: A Governor's Guide to Supporting a Comprehensive High-Quality Early Childhood State System" (Washington, D.C.: The National Governors Association Center for Best Practices, 2010), 3–4.
17. The Campaign for Grade-Level Reading, http://www.gradelevelreading.net/ (accessed October 2011). IMLS has become a formal partner of the Campaign and has made its goals a focus in the National Leadership Grant program.
18. Institute of Museum and Library Services, "Let's Move! Museums and Gardens," http://www.imls.gov/about/letsmove.aspx (accessed October 2011).

About the Author

Marsha L. Semmel is Director, Office of Strategic Partnerships, at the Institute of Museum and Library Services, a federal agency based in Washington, DC. She has been president and CEO of Conner Prairie, a living history museum near Indianapolis, and Women of the West Museum, in Denver. She worked at the National Endowment for the Humanities (NEH) for twelve years, where, from 1993–1996, she directed the NEH Division of Public Programs. This article was written in Ms. Semmel's personal capacity. The views expressed are her own and do not necessarily represent the views of the Institute of Museum and Library Services, or the United States Government.

Integrating Scaffolding Experiences for the Youngest Visitors in Museums

Barbara Wolf and Elizabeth Wood

Abstract Research demonstrates that children have vast potential to expand their knowledge base with simple supports from adults and older children. Children's museums have a heightened awareness of the value in and the need to reach out to support adults accompanying children, thus bringing about an emphasis on family learning. Iterative exhibition studies conducted at The Children's Museum of Indianapolis illustrate the impact of planning for family learning. But for any museum, intentionally applying the strategy of scaffolding by building on simple concepts and working toward mastery of ideas, can inform adults and simultaneously help children stretch to new levels of understanding and achievement. This strategy requires curators, educators and exhibit developers to work collaboratively to determine various levels of accessibility of content and activity moving from entry level ideas through more complex and abstract ones for older children and adults.

Children visiting museums of all types is certainly nothing new, but their experience in those spaces has changed over time. From the earliest iterations of children's museums, to contemporary practices in museums of all types, the attention museum professionals place on the needs of this special audience is changing. The idea of hands-on learning, facilitated and mediated learning experiences, and scaled-down environments have become more prominent (and often expected) in museum settings where young children visit with their families. The increased visitation of family groups, especially those with young children, requires greater attention by museum educators, exhibition developers, and designers to support the learning needs of this audience. Most children's museums place special emphasis on designing environments that support learning for very young children. Lessons learned from the work done in children's museums can provide models for those in other museum settings to meet the needs of early learners.

Journal of Museum Education, Volume 37, Number 1, Spring 2012, pp. 29–38.

Children's museums acknowledge that providing for early learners, ranging from babies as young as three months to five year-old preschoolers, is an essential aspect of their mission. Typically, museum exhibitions apply constructivist learning approaches wherein children generate knowledge by connecting experiences in exhibitions and specialized environments to their own ideas. While limited, the research in children's museums that has emerged from these experiences tends to center on the following two foci, often concurrently: defining what early learning looks like in children's museums and exploring the role of adults in these early learning experiences.

Several studies conducted at the Please Touch Museum in Philadelphia and Harvard's Project Zero in Cambridge investigated not only *if* young children learn at children's museum exhibitions, but also *what* they learn. In addition, these collected studies examined the role of adult guidance in children's learning.[1] Researchers used observed children as they interacted with exhibit components and subsequently coded their behaviors to find patterns. Based on the types of behaviors displayed, researchers categorized behaviors into discrete types of learning such as factual, procedural, or cause and effect. Findings suggest that children are indeed learning in exhibitions and environments at children's museums and that learning is comprised of far more than the acquisition of facts and disciplinary content knowledge, and extends into developmental areas such as procedural and cause and effect learning. Moreover, positive effects on children's learning cycles clearly emerged as an outcome of active adult guidance.

Family Learning in Children's Museums

A movement away from child-centered experiences and toward family-centered experiences has slowly permeated the collective attention of leaders in children's museums. Administrators, planners, and developers have addressed the obvious: the majority of very young children cannot come to museums without adult accompaniment. In using child-centered approaches museum professionals realized that they were overlooking the adults as critical members of the learning cohort and that incorporating them into learning events offered the potential to expand the experience beyond the museum. Given this actuality, children's museums have heightened awareness of the value in and the need to reach out to support adults accompanying children, thus bringing about an emphasis on family learning. In these museums, planning to bring about family learning outcomes is intentional; goals and objectives for family learning outcomes are integrated into the development process from beginning to end. Although nascent, the body of research related to family learning is the most robust area of study related to early learning in children's museums.

One noteworthy study confirmed the essential role parents and caregivers play in guiding and supporting children's learning experiences in children's museums.[2] Researchers in that study found that children who received open-ended questioning ("vague guidance") from their parent/care-giver resulted in increased learning compared to children who received no guidance or prescriptive guidance (e.g., adult told answers or correct solutions) at exhibit components.

Despite the evident positive correlation between children's learning and parental involvement, several studies found that there is an apparent misalignment between parents' and children's museum professionals' expectations and beliefs about how young children learn and adults' roles in guiding that learning.[3] For instance, one study found that in an exhibition designed to promote parent-child pretend play interactions, parents' seeming discomfort with and lack of buy-in to the importance of pretend-play limited their involvement instead prompting them to assume a more didactic teaching role rather than engage in imaginative play. Other studies identified various cultural differences and preferences, as well as obstacles to parent involvement in children's museums, including a lack of understanding of the importance of play in young children's learning, a preference to simply watch their children play or a hesitance to play in public.[4] The sum of these studies' findings suggest that parents' beliefs about young children's learning and their role in that learning is often divergent from those espoused by museum professionals, and/or parents simply do not know how best to support or guide their young child's learning. Because parental involvement and guidance appear to increase young children's learning, further inquiry by children's museum professionals is necessary to bridge the gap between parents' intrinsic attitudes and beliefs about learning and how to design experiences to elicit family learning and engagement.[5] This must come along with the acknowledgement that families choose to visit the museum for a variety of reasons. Paying attention to these motivations is useful in designing experiences that meet a wide range of interests and expectations.

Research at The Children's Museum of Indianapolis

Over the past ten years, The Children's Museum of Indianapolis has developed and refined its family learning initiatives and strategies.[6] This work included an institution-wide demonstrable shift away from child-centered experiences, to those where families (defined as at least one adult and one child with an on-going relationship) collaborate on problems, enhance the experience through personal connection, and build on each other's participation. Various strategies used by museum staff in numerous departments involved in exhibition and program development have been built over time. In recent years they have become the basis for multiple studies on the effects and implications of family learning at the museum.

Research strategies include the triangulation of data collected from observations of families in situ, data from timing and tracking of these same family units, post-visit interviews and post-visit online surveys, the latter gathered after a one year interval. Unique to these studies is a design that required trained observers to follow the same family from the beginning to the end of their entire experience in an exhibition. The most recent studies have been conducted in galleries that were explicitly designed according to family learning principles. Research and evaluation studies conducted across exhibitions since 2007 have yielded several replicated findings; the generalizability of these findings holds promise for other museums that intentionally integrate family learning cues for adults.[7]

A shared understanding among staff is that the amount of time a family has apportioned for their visit is a primary driver of their experience. A corollary assumption and ultimately a hypothesis to the iterative research conducted is that the greater the amount of time a family spends in an intentionally designed space provides greater *opportunity* for learning to occur. While this assumption has certain intuitive appeal, recent findings on interactive learning behaviors between parent and child have affirmed this convincingly. Comparing visit duration in the initial family learning exhibition, *Dinosphere: Now You Are in Their World* to the most recent, *Take Me There: Egypt*, indicates that visit duration is increasing. Immersive environments are particularly effective in contributing to lengthened visits and stimulation of learning interactions between adults and children.

Increase in the length of an exhibition visit is even greater when comparing a family learning based exhibition with pre-2007 exhibitions that did not employ this strategy. Regardless of exhibition content, the distribution of families studied consistently clustered into three identifiable groups based on length of visit. These groups represent particular, observable behaviors of the family that revealed differences in the type and number of learning interactions associated with each group. In three of the four family learning based exhibitions those who remained the longest comprised more than 54% of the families in the study sample. When looking at individual components of exhibitions and holding power varies, but more importantly, popularity of an exhibit component is not a perfect correlation with time spent at a component. Moreover, the correlation between the absolute number of components in an exhibition area and stay time is weak: more exhibit components are not predictive of longer stay times.

Using an inventory of 54 learning behavior interactions indicative of Participatory, Problem Solving/Collaborative or Enhancement interactions, the narratives of the observations were coded. Those families with long stay times had the highest average number of interactions. They distributed their interactions almost equally between Participation and Enhancement and engaged in Problem Solving/Collaboration more so than did those families that visited for shorter periods.

The question of whether or not visitors read labels has long been discussed in the museum field. For the *Take Me There: Egypt* exhibition, curators, exhibition/content developers and designers purposefully integrated the family learning strategy of scaffolding in the texts and into the associated exhibit components. In the subsequent study of the exhibition, when families were anonymously surveyed on whether or not they found the family learning exhibit labels helpful to their understanding and their overall exhibition experience, the overwhelming majority (97%) agreed that the labels were at least "Helpful" with a large proportion (57%) indicating that they were "Very helpful." Respondents had the option to reply that the labels were "Not helpful at all" (1%) or, "I didn't read them" (2%). These results suggest that because the majority of families were reading the labels, doing so is likely to have contributed to increased stay time to some extent.

Scaffolding in Children's Museums' Exhibitions

At its most basic, scaffolding (for any learner) requires simplification of ideas or tasks and encouraging the learner toward successful experiences with that idea or task.[8] Scaffolded experiences are temporary. The adult role in scaffolding children's learning experiences occurs when the adult or parent recognizes that some additional form of support, guidance, or resources is needed to help the child move toward understanding, independent learning or mastery of that task or concept.

Parent involvement and interactions with their children in support of learning can occur across multiple settings and a wide range of experiences. In various settings, particularly those that have not been intentionally designed for young children, parents and other adults may naturally scaffold the learning and interactions of children. For example, consider a simple visit to a grocery store with a young child. The child has been to the store many times with an adult. The child knows the basic patterns of a shopping trip: select items, put them in the cart, pay the cashier and put the items in a bag. On this particular visit, the child wants to help. Her father might allow her to pay the cashier. The child knows that she must do something with the money. Father may hand his daughter the money and continue to guide her through the process: "Hand the money to the cashier. Okay, now get your change." Even the adult cashier can scaffold the experience. She might say, "That will be five dollars and ten cents, please!" This type of adult involvement allows the child a level of autonomy while at the same time helping her to learn the process. Soon enough, she'll be able to do this on her own. For the most part, the scaffolding experiences that adults provide stem from common collective knowledge of situations and scenarios that contribute to children's overall learning.

In children's museum settings, parents are inherently predisposed to a focus on children. The decision to visit a children's museum probably came from an adult expectation or hope to provide a meaningful learning experience for their children, or simply for a family outing.[9] The adults can enter, fairly assured, that the experiences and learning opportunities at a children's museum will be geared toward their child specifically. Yet even in these specially designed environments, parents may still need to provide scaffolding that is unique to their own children's stage of development, their interests, or their abilities. Parent interactions with children in these settings may reflect various needs of their children ranging from scaffolding of more abstract concepts by providing more information, such as how far away Egypt might be, or to support developmental experiences, such as encouraging the child in a sorting or classification activity.

An example of exhibit-based scaffolding demonstrates how an activity designed for toddlers can support messages for a gallery targeted for much older youth. *The Power of Children: Making a Difference* exhibition at The Children's Museum of Indianapolis, tells the story of prejudice and intolerance through the stories of Anne Frank, Ruby Bridges and Ryan White. One of the central messages of the exhibition is that children have the power to fight intolerance through their words, actions, and their voice. For very young children these messages are difficult to deliver — even for a parent. The "Kindness Tree" is a simple activity for parents and young children to work on together. The tree, with a metal trunk and just a few branches, has multiple magnetic "leaves" that can be placed in any configuration. On each leaf are words with illustrated acts of kindness. These include simple ideas such as, "Let others go first" and "Sit with someone new." The child can easily add leaves to the tree or rearrange them. The parent scaffolds the experience by reading the messages and relating those experiences to the child as he or she completes the activity.

Implications and Call to Action

Planning and development of environments that support learning for all ages in *any* type of museum requires careful consideration of both the probable content knowledge and abilities of the children and adults in the visiting audience. Already, many history and art museums and science centers have developed valuable and focused strategies to support the needs of family visitors and specifically younger children (see for example the cases presented in the Family Learning Forum, a project with the USS Constitution Museum, and McRainey & Russick's *Connecting Kids to History with Museum Exhibitions*). There is great interest in the museum field for more intentional efforts to continue this effort and build meaningful and appropriate spaces for families with young children. This forethought requires curators, educators, exhibition and program developers as well as designers to work collaboratively to home in on key features of content or activity that can interest and stimulate various levels of interaction by visitors. These might represent small-scale efforts such as family guides or larger-scale endeavors like a family-friendly exhibition space.

Given that parents might naturally scaffold some part of the learning experience for their child, exhibition planners and designers can build on these tendencies to promote further and better learning for even the youngest audiences. Rather than adding on a separate area for the littlest visitors (although this does have its place in certain experiences), the *content* of an exhibition can be scrutinized for potential opportunities for scaffolding. On a broader level, institutions might consider developing an overall plan across exhibitions to meet family learning goals and objectives: essentially, what would we like to have happen and where. This strategy requires curators and exhibition developers to determine various levels of accessibility of content moving from entry level ideas through more complex and abstract ones for older children and adults. Such ideas can be developed in multiple ways using learning frameworks that provide age-specific details on cognitive abilities, characteristics of age groups, and capacity of children in different content areas by age.[10] By applying these developmental frameworks appropriate scaffolding can support even the youngest children in an exhibition that might not be specifically targeted for their age group. Unique formats can also be offered. The Art Institute of Chicago caters to parents of very young children (18 months or younger) by offering guided stroller tours. During the stroller tours on such topics as Impressionism or Modern Art parents receive tips and strategies for how to provide and scaffold art experiences for their children; the tour ends in a "family room" where participants can engage in art-centered activities that are developmentally appropriate for young learners. Regardless of the approach taken, it is vital to observe and collect data on whether the approach achieves the intended outcomes. The scaffolding provided should be an engaging, diverse, and balanced approach to stimulate interactions, rather than didactic instructions that parents may perceive as arduous.

Other intentional planning of learning experiences (e.g., age appropriate curator carts, live actor interpretations, accessible educators or simple applications of mobile cellular technology) especially those for young children not only supports their learning, but also provides clues, contexts and even nudges for adults to provide scaffolding. Family members (whether parents or older siblings) will then move more comfortably to support younger children in successful navigation of museum experiences, especially when in environments that are not designed with children in mind.

In contrast to children's museums, those museums where the content and context are focused on older audiences, the need for scaffolding is considerable since as Marilyn Burns posited: children are not "short adults".[11] The most fruitful strategies for these museums to take are to understand the range of content potential, as well as the cognitive and physical capabilities of the youngest visitors. Scaffolding does not need to entail a full-scale reinvention of every gallery space. Instead, many museums can elect to highlight particular aspects of the collection that may have more appeal to younger visitors, or that lend themselves to differentiation by levels of complexity. Research demonstrates that children have vast potential to expand their knowledge base with simple supports from adults and older children. By building on simple concepts, and working toward mastery of ideas, scaffolding in any museum can inform adults and simultaneously help children stretch to new levels of understanding and achievement.

Acknowledgements

Special thanks to Camille Warren for her assistance on preparing the manuscript.

Notes

1. Nancy T. Haas. "Project Explore: How Children are Really Learning in Children's Museums." *The Visitor Studies Association* 9, no. 1 (1997): 63–69; Laurel Puchner, Robyn Rapoport and Suzanne Gaskins. "Learning in Children's Museums: Is it Really Happening?" *Curator: The Museum Journal* 44, no. 3 (2001): 237–259; Robert Russell L. "Project Explore: Please Touch Museum and Harvard University's Project Zero." *Informal Learning* 37 (Summer 1999): 1, 4–5.
2. Haas. "Project Explore: How Children are Really Learning in Children's Museums."

3. Stephanie Downey, Amanda Krantz and Emily Skidmore. "The Parental Role in Children's Museums." *Museums and Social Issues* 5, no. 1 (2010): 15–34; Suzanne Gaskins. "The Cultural Meaning of Play and Learning in Children's Museums." *Hand to Hand* 22, no. 4 (Winter 2008): 1–2, 8–11; Stephanie Shine and Teresa Y. Acosta. "Parent-Child Social Play in a Children's Museum." *Family Relations* 49, no. 1 (January 2000): 45–52; Mallary I. Swartz and Kevin Crowley. "Parent Beliefs about Teaching and Learning in a Children's Museum." *Visitor Studies Today* 7, no. 2 (Summer 2004): 1, 5–16.
4. Downey. "The Parental Role in Children's Museums;" Gaskins. "The Cultural Meaning of Play and Learning in Children's Museums;" Elizabeth Wood and Barbara Wolf. "When Parents Stand Back is Family Learning Still Possible?" *Museums and Social Issues* 5, no. 1 (2010): 35–50.
5. Elizabeth Wood and Barbara Wolf. "Between the Lines of Engagement in Museums." *Journal of Museum Education* 33, no. 2 (2008): 121–130.
6. Wood. "When Parents Stand Back is Family Learning Still Possible?"
7. Barbara Wolf. "The Nature of Research and Evaluation in Children's Museums: Some Recommendations for Determining Generalizability." *Hand to Hand* 3, no. 1 (1989): 1, 9.
8. David Wood, Jerome Bruner, and Gail Ross. "The Role of Tutoring in Problem Solving." *Journal of Child Psychiatry and Psychology* 17, no. 2 (1976): 89–100.
9. Susie Wilkening and James Chung. "The Challenge of Moms." *Life Stages of the Museum Visitor* (Washington, DC: AAM Press, 2009).
10. Elizabeth Reich Rawson. "It's About Them: Using Developmental Frameworks to Create Exhibitions for Children (and Their Grown-Ups)." *Connecting Kids to History with Museum Exhibitions*, ed. D. L. McRainey and J. Russick (Walnut Creek, CA: Left Coast Press, 2010).
11. Marilyn Burns. *I Am Not a Short Adult: Getting Good at Being a Kid* (Covelo, CA: Yolla Bolly Press, 1997).

About the Authors

Barbara Wolf, PhD, is Associate Vice President of Research and Family Learning Evaluation at The Children's Museum of Indianapolis; she is also a Distinguished Professor of Teaching and Professor Emeritus of Education and Evaluation Studies at Indiana University, Bloomington. Her work focuses on process learning and outcomes measurement.

Elizabeth Wood, PhD, is an associate professor of museum studies and teacher education at Indiana University-Purdue University Indianapolis and public scholar of museums, families, and learning at The Children's Museum of Indianapolis. Her research and evaluation work focuses on critical museum pedagogy and object-based learning.

A Look at Early Childhood Programming in Museums

Betsy Bowers

Abstract Based on data from an exploratory, online survey, this article reveals that a surprisingly high number of art and history museums currently offer programs for very young children. The author describes the kinds of challenges that survey respondents faced when planning and conducting programs, and calls for more research and more collective action.

Young Children and Museums

Not so long ago it was only the most adventurous museum educator who would present a gallery-based experience to a group of three and four year olds. Although many museums recognize the value of early learning in museums, some still wonder whether young children belong in a traditional art, history or science museum. At a time when videos keep our kids occupied during long car rides and action games with avatars play on TVs in our living rooms, museum educators recognize how important it is for young learners to connect with what's "real." Authentic objects have the potential to inspire awe, promote wonder and encourage curiosity. Over 30 years ago, Bruno Bettelheim phrased it in this way:

> This, then, I believe to be the museum's greatest value to the child irrespective of what a museum's content may be: to stimulate his imagination, to arouse his curiosity so that he wishes to penetrate ever more deeply the meaning of what he is exposed to in the museum, to give him a chance to admire in his own good time things which are beyond his

Journal of Museum Education, Volume 37, Number 1, Spring 2012, pp. 39–48.

> ken, and most important of all, to give him a feeling of awe for the wonder of the world. Because a world that is not full of wonder is one hardly worth the effort of growing up in. [1]

This sense of wonder is evident in the lives of young children. If you know a child that's under age five, you know that he or she is naturally filled with wonder, curiosity, and questions. He learns by exploring, creating, experimenting, and doing. He learns from stories and real life experiences. History museums are about stories and real life experiences. Science museums are about experimenting. Art museums are about creating. More and more museums are finding that when presented appropriately, even the most humble object, artifact, or masterpiece can become an opportunity for a young child to discover and construct meaning and new knowledge.

Advocates of "environment as teacher" recognize that museum galleries and exhibitions inspire awe. Beauty, light, reflection, transparency and design form the essence of many museums. Early childhood educators in Reggio Emilia, Italy, were the first to show that very young children respond positively and thoughtfully when surrounded by things of beauty,[2] and educators recognize the positive influence that the environment can have on a child's learning experience. When museum educators help young children become acquainted with and comfortable in gallery spaces, object centered exhibitions and interesting architectural areas, opportunities for building life-long learning skills and a strong aesthetic sense emerge.

The Time is Now

Although early childhood education is drawing national attention, museums have been slow to show how they collectively contribute to early learning. In May 2011, the Obama administration announced funding for the "Early Learning Challenge." According to Education Secretary Arne Duncan, "To win the future, our children need a strong start." In addition, he stated, "The Race to the Top-Early Learning Challenge encourages states to develop bold and comprehensive plans for raising the quality of early learning programs across America."[3] Research indicating the importance of early learning on an individual's success in school and long term achievement[4] contributed to this initiative.

Many museums are already engaging our nation's youngest learners alongside their parents, caregivers and teachers and some are aligning their programs with learning standards defined for young children. An organized effort to compile and present research in support of early learning in object centered museums would contribute to the field's understanding of how to develop the best early childhood programs possible. The art and artifacts in museum collections can contribute important foundation skills[5] in language, math, science and social studies that lead to children's future success in school.

An Exploratory Survey

To get a sense of what museums are doing to accommodate young audiences, I developed and posted an online exploratory survey on a museum educator listserv. The questions I asked were general and designed to determine current interests in early childhood programs in museums: What kinds of museums are accommodating what age audiences? How are early childhood programs structured and assessed and what challenges are being encountered? In order to encourage participation, I asked questions that were simple and straightforward. Respondents could complete the survey in as little as ten minutes.

The survey results provide an initial look at the state of early childhood education in museums. It serves as a place to start a conversation and suggests opportunities for further data collection and study.

This exploratory survey comes at a time of a great deal of interest in measuring the effectiveness of museum experiences on audiences. It builds upon work conducted at science museums and other organizations interested in informal learning in the sciences. The National Science Foundation and U.S. Department of Education have provided infrastructural models and funding for some of these evaluation projects and have made findings easily available.[6] The Association of Children's Museums is another organization that has taken the lead on assessing early learning. Information on its website includes statistical data and research.[7] But otherwise, research and evaluation related to very young audiences in more traditional object-focused museums is hard to find.

Nearly seventy individuals responded to the online survey, and surprisingly, the vast majority indicated that their museums provide programming for very young visitors. Those who responded primarily represent art (34) and history (23) museums.

The ten-question survey included nine multiple-choice questions. One additional open-ended question requested the survey taker to identify his or her type of institution. Completed surveys represent a variety of museum disciplines including historic sites and history, art, culture, science and children's museums. Of the 69 respondents that completed the survey, 88% provide programming for children younger than kindergarten age and about 50% serve children under the age of two. Of the ten museums providing infant programming, five of those are art museums. Many of these programs have just started in the past five years but of those museums that have had programming for the past several years, a few indicated that they recently restructured or added new programs to better accommodate their visitors' interests. Since many of these programs have started only recently, opportunities to share experiences and develop a common set of best practices are important next steps. This will help museum educators more effectively advocate for museums as meaningful educational resources for early learners.

Most of the museums that serve young visitors conduct programs for children *and* parents. These programs are most often designed and implemented by museum educators. Survey results indicate that early childhood programs are staffed in a variety of ways. Two common staffing patterns emerged in the survey: 1) one museum teacher leading a group or 2) one teacher supported by an assistant teacher or volunteer. Since many of the programs do not require preregistration, it can be difficult to plan effectively. Most survey responses suggest that the number of program participants does not influence the number of staff or volunteers that support program implementation. Although not made clear from survey results, it is possible that museum educators see parents as able to provide an adult-child ratio that supports successful learning experiences. On the other hand, this situation might suggest that museums that offer early childhood programming face a staffing challenge. Both circumstances can be problematic and worth additional exploration, for research in early childhood education indicates that quality experiences depend on high educator to student ratios.

Survey participants indicated that the second most significant challenge they face is finding time to prepare programs. It can be a time-consuming process to organize developmentally appropriate hands-on activities that accommodate different learning styles. However, experienced early childhood educators know to use techniques to engage young learners that don't always require extensive preparation. Museum educators new to early childhood learning may want to collaborate with experts in the field. For example, if museum educators partner with university programs specializing in early childhood education, early childhood educators could share their expertise and provide insight on how to balance planning, preparation and implementation that result in effective learning experiences. In return, museum educators can provide their academic partners with opportunities for undergraduate and graduate students to study early childhood learning in museums. For institutions offering degrees in museum education, experiences like these could not only support early childhood programs, but could also help their students better understand an important museum audience.

In addition to the challenges already stated, 30% of the surveys indicated that there are other challenges as well. The survey did not allow respondents to define these other challenges, but the response suggests a need to establish a platform for idea sharing and problem solving related specifically to early learning in museums.

For museums to be able to sustain programs for young children, assessing effectiveness is also an important challenge. Survey takers shared information about how they determine if their early childhood programs are successful. Eighty-six percent indicated that program success is determined by the "level of audience engagement." Other indicators of success include ease of activity flow (69%), full enrollment (59%), parent survey responses (51%), and measuring achievement of program objectives by participants (48%). Although full program enrollment and these other factors are important for sustaining programs, consistent determination of whether program objectives are achieved will result in a level of credibility that will serve the field well. Ultimately, for museums to receive attention and support at a national level, educators will need to prove that programs support children's success in school and long term achievement. The process has started with research related to family learning in museums. At least two aspects of work in this area could influence how museum educators approach evaluative efforts. Family learning research can help museum educators more clearly define early learning in museums and help identify what questions are most important to address.[8] Eleven surveyed museums indicated that their early childhood programs are assessed by external evaluators. It would be useful to find out more about these museums and the programs that are being formally evaluated.

Overall, the results of this exploratory survey indicate that there is enough interest in young audiences to warrant a larger and more thorough evaluation of early childhood programming in museums. More data could provide the field with a deeper understanding of early learning in museums and its impact on young learners. For example: How are the diverse learning needs of very young learners being accommodated? What is it that museum educators hope to achieve in their programs for children under the age of five? How are museum educators supporting parents to ensure a positive and effective family experience in the museum? What kinds of activities are museums providing for infant audiences? How do programs accommodate individuals with varying abilities and backgrounds? What kind of long-term impact do our programs for young children have on these individuals as they enter school and grow into adults?

Current Practices of Early Childhood Gallery-Based Programs

It is exciting that museums recognize the benefits of museums as avenues of learning for young children. Although this survey did not collect detailed information about the kinds of activities and experiences museums provide for early childhood audiences, a few respondents offered additional information. It is worth noting the variety of experiences that museums offer. The following paragraphs present just a few.

The Newark Museum has collaborated with community organizations to provide developmentally appropriate gallery-based experiences in conjunction with a past exhibition entitled *Constructive Spirit: Abstract Art in South and North America, 1920s — 1950s.* By collaborating with the early childhood education and Spanish speaking community, the museum focused content on important foundational learning concepts, such as shape, line, and color. The museum's approach took into account some basic principles of learning theory such as the relevance of developmental psychologist Howard Gardner's multiple intelligences and David Ausubel's ideas about advance organizers. By providing the Pre-K teachers with pre-museum activity materials in advance, children are better prepared to make meaningful connections to museum experiences once they arrive. In addition to providing Pre-K classroom teachers with pre and post-activity information and ideas, an artist in residence incorporated music and movement into the experience, engaging kinesthetic learners. Based on this original model, the program continues to evolve. Given that the program attracted twice the number anticipated, the need and interest for this type of programming is apparent, and the funder is continuing to support the partnership.[9]

To encourage young children to love history and enjoy learning about it, the Missouri History Museum uses a different approach to engage young audiences. Its "Storytelling in the Museum" program uses traditional and contemporary stories and craft projects to engage children between the ages of two and five with artifacts on display. In the book, *Connecting Kids to History with Museum Exhibitions,* museum educator Leslie Bedford explains that storytelling "engages listeners' imaginations and emotions, and thus their memories."[10] The Missouri History Museum uses dramatic narrative with both large and small groups of children to explore its collection and stimulate the children's interest in artifacts. In addition to "Storytelling at the Museum," the museum offers a program called "Parent & Me," in which families sign up for up to four 90-minute themed classes that connect to different exhibitions. Families with children ages two to five years old move throughout gallery and classroom spaces at their own pace, engaging in playful activities designed by museum educators that incorporate touch, movement, smell, music, knowledge of basic shapes and colors, art, and more. Staff members at the museum believe that these early childhood experiences contribute to a lifelong habit of visiting museums.

Museum educators at the Smithsonian Early Enrichment Center, a museum-based preschool program located at the Smithsonian on the National Mall, find ways to engage young learners in traditional museum exhibitions. By using strategies that connect very young children (between the ages of eight months and six years) with museum collections, students become comfortable in the museum and build skills critical for their later success in K–12 school settings. Teaching techniques include using touchable objects familiar to the children to connect them to artifacts and stories of people from around the world. In June 2011, the two and three-year-olds were introduced to West African culture though a well-known summer drink, lemonade. Beginning with the children's book, *Lulu's Lemonade*, by Barbara Derubertis, they went on to examine and discuss the art work *Zinnias and a Blue Dish with Lemons*, by Charles Demuth. They took an imaginary shopping excursion in the food market exhibit in the National Museum of Natural History's *African Voices* and returned to school to make their own version of West African lemonade complete with lemons, sugar, ginger, cayenne, water and ice.[11]

Museum educators are taught to use informal learning environments to build critical thinking skills in visitors of all ages. By applying what learning theorists such as John Dewey, Lev Vygotsky, Jean Piaget, and Howard Gardner say about how young children learn, creative gallery-based experiences can result in increased learning and future academic achievement. As these examples indicate, museum educators have opportunities to use traditional museum resources to prepare young children for success in school. Additional research, shared throughout the field, will contribute to the development of programs that make the best use of museums and establish a much-needed foundation for best practices.

Increasing Young Audiences Through Collaboration and Research

Although informal, results from this on-line survey suggest that museum educators recognize the significance of early learning in museums. Enough museums are providing program opportunities to young children to warrant additional research and a larger conversation that allow program planners to learn from one another and continue to improve collection-focused experiences. A community of educators that works together to share information about early childhood programming in museums would contribute to future program effectiveness and garner national attention. Survey results indicate that the challenges are many. They range from difficulties with the registration process, to the lack of time to prepare for the activity, finding staff to support the success of the experience, and getting support from colleagues and departments in the museum. Only a handful of respondents, though, indicated that they were challenged by "maintaining focus and control in the galleries." Not only does this suggest that young children are not the disruptive audiences that some museum administrators fear, but it also suggests that museums have a clear indication that museums can work for this age group.

In conclusion, preliminary findings indicate that we need to follow up and gather additional evidence that will help decision-makers in our institutions, in the educational system, and in the government recognize the importance of early learning and the positive impact museums can have. It is time for museum educators and early childhood educators to work together, and it is time for museum educators to work with one another to provide evidence that substantiates what so many already know; museums are rich with opportunities for children in the earliest stage of their lifelong learning experience.

Notes

1. Bruno Bettelheim, Ph.D., "Children, Curiosity and Museums." *Roundtable Report*, vol. 5., no. 2 (1979): 8 — 13.
2. Carolyn Edwards, Lella Gandini and George Forman, *The Hundred Languages of Children: The Reggio Emilia Approach to Early Childhood Education*, (New Jersey: Ablex Publishing Corporation, 1993), 140.
3. U.S. Department of Health and Human Services, "Obama Administration Announces $500 Million for Race to the Top — Early Learning Challenge," HHS Press Office, May 25, 2011, http://www.hhs.gov/news/press/2011pres/05/20110525a.html, (accessed June 1, 2011).
4. Arthur Reynolds, PhD., and others, "Long-term Effects of an Early Childhood Intervention on Educational Achievement and Juvenile Arrest," *The Journal of the American Medical Association*, 2001.
5. Sharon Shaffer, PhD, *The Museum Connection: A Field Guide for Educators of Children 3 – 7 Years*, (Washington, DC: Smithsonian Early Enrichment Center, 2010), 11.
6. A. Friedman, (ED.). *Framework for Evaluating Impacts of Informal Science Education Projects*, 2008.
7. Association of Childrens Museums. www.childrensmuseums.org/demo/index.php?option=com_content&view=article&id=87&Itemid=93.
8. John H. Falk, Lynn D. Dierking and Susan Foutz, eds. *In Principle, In Practice: Museums as Learning Institutions*, (Lanham, MD: Alta Mira Press, 2007), 17–30.

9. Ted Lind, "Museum Learning: More Than Meets the Eye," *Educational Viewpoints: The Journal of the New Jersey Principals and Supervisors Association*, 2011.
10. D. Lynn McRainey and John Russick, eds. *Connecting Kids to History with Museum Exhibitions*, (Walnut Creek, CA: Left Coast Press, 2010), 100 – 103.
11. Danielle Lacroix, Smithsonian Early Enrichment Center Interpretive Plan, "Around the World: Lemonade," June 2011.

About the Author

Betsy Bowers, Deputy Director of Collaborations, Partnerships and Consulting at the Smithsonian Early Enrichment Center, started her career in early childhood education. She is a graduate of The George Washington University Museum Education Program and current adjunct faculty member. She worked for many years as a Qm2 consultant, advising the National Building Museum, National Law Enforcement Museum, Hillwood Estate, Museum and Gardens, Roanoke Island Festival Park, among others.

Museum Superheroes

The Role of Play in Young Children's Lives

Pamela Krakowski

Abstract This article explores the role of play in an art museum. Reflecting upon a kindergarten field trip to the Warhol Museum in which children's play was the centerpiece of the museum experience, the author examines what early childhood theorists have written about the value of play in young children's lives. She shows how the Warhol's program for young children makes use of the theorists' concepts of active engagement, intrinsic motivation, identity formation, symbolic thought, and memory-in-action, and concludes that play can be an effective strategy for stimulating young minds in museums of all types.

> When children pretend, they aren't limited to the way things are in the real world. They're using their imaginations to move beyond the bounds of reality. A stick can be a magic wand. A sock can be a puppet. A small child can be a powerful superhero, a crying baby, a mean dragon, or a scary lion — whatever he or she wants to be. — *Fred Rogers*[1]

Play is a natural mode of learning for young children. Children play to make sense of their world and everything in it. While play is most likely associated with doll houses and trucks in a home or school environment, it is important to expand our thinking about play and consider how it can support learning in other environments, even museums.

Writers, theorists, and researchers tell us that play has an essential role in children's intellectual, psychological, and social development. The intent of this

Journal of Museum Education, Volume 37, Number 1, Spring 2012, pp. 49–58.

article is to explore the role of play in an art museum. I do this by reflecting upon a kindergarten field trip to the Warhol Museum in which the children's play was the centerpiece of the museum experience. To better understand play's role, I examine what theorists have written about the value of play in children's lives.

The Museum Experience

> When Elliott got home from school, he took all of the pillows off his living room couch and jumped on top of them, shouting, "I'm Super Tree Frog!" Adjusting his yellow superhero cape that he designed that morning at The Warhol, he climbed back on the couch and took another daring leap into the air. Anyone watching Elliott that afternoon would have seen a brightly-colored, silkscreened portrait of Andy Warhol on the back of his cape.[2]

In the spring of 2010, the kindergarten teachers at the Falk Laboratory School, and myself, the children's art teacher, met with museum educators from the Warhol to discuss a possible collaboration between our two organizations.[3] We both wanted to create a museum experience that would be meaningful and age appropriate for kindergarten. After talking in depth about the children's interests, their current play themes, and the Warhol collection, everyone agreed upon the theme of superheroes. We would use images from Warhol's Myth series.

A few days before our field trip, the museum educators came to our school for their pre-visit. Through an interactive presentation, they engaged the kindergarteners in a conversation about Andy Warhol growing up in Pittsburgh, making connections to the children's everyday experiences. They shared some of the images that the children would encounter on their field trip, such as Superman and the Wicked Witch from the *Wizard of Oz*. And then, like Clark Kent changing into superman in a phone booth, they hid inside a closet, and magically reappeared wearing yellow capes and matching eye masks. On the back of their capes were silkscreened images of Andy Warhol — similar to what the children would be creating. As one would have imagined, the children could not contain their excitement. That very day all of the children received their own capes and began their "underpainting" for the silkscreen they would continue to make in the museum's art studio — the Factory. The next time they saw their capes was on the day of our field trip.

The children arrived at the Warhol with high anticipation. Each activity contained a surprise — silkscreening their capes and seeing the image immediately appear, putting on their capes and imagining super powers, wearing 3-D glasses and seeing flowers pop out of paintings. For each activity the museum educators used a playful approach to engage the children with a work of art. For example, when the children visited Warhol's *Elvis*, they were invited to share their thoughts, feelings and perceptions. Then the educators played music from Elvis' era. The children as superheroes created their own movements, dancing with *Elvis* and each other.

For three hours, 44 kindergarteners remained engaged. When the field trip was over, the children returned to school and wore their capes for the rest of the day, on the buses home, at home, and to bed. The next day they arrived back at school wearing their capes, ready to play.

A Year Later. . .

A year later, reflecting on this experience, I decided to invite the kindergarteners — now in first grade — to bring their capes to art class. Sitting with the children on the art studio floor, I invited them to share their memories about their museum visit and to talk about how they used their capes. Collectively, they gave a detailed account of every hands-on activity, beginning with Tara describing the exact sequence of how to silkscreen a superhero cape — which for her, she clarified, "was a cape for a fairy princess." They talked animatedly for more than an hour. I wrote down what they shared.[4]

"I remember we all sat on this BIG white couch and pretended we were on top of a mountain. The bad guys couldn't get to us."

"That picture of the witch scared me sooooo much. And then I remembered I was safe 'cause I had my cape on."

"When I saw all those soup boxes, I said to myself, 'Wow! They look like a fort.' I went home and I looked around for boxes and I built my own fort."

"My parents and I went back to the museum. I wore my cape and took my parents to the pillow room. I could be 'it' because I had the cape on. I could tag them because I had the special powers of the cape. And then the pillows floated down and anyone who got hit by a pillow was 'it.'

"We sat in front of these paintings with flowers, and when we put these 3-D glasses on, the flowers popped out. I tried looking at other paintings, but it only worked with the flower painting."

"They took us to this long, long painting with a rock star holding a blaster," began Matt.

"That was Elvis," interrupted Sam.

"Yeah, it was Elvis," continued Matt. "And they played this music and we danced with Elvis. It was fun."

"Yeah, it was really fun," agreed Sam.

As the children spoke, I was struck by how vivid their memories were and by how excited they were — even a year later. I remembered how actively engaged they were during the field trip and how play was embedded within all of the activities. I wanted to understand the role of play in engaging the children and making the experience meaningful, so I turned to early childhood education literature on play.

Play and its Characteristics

"How can you tell if it is play?' is a question that has been asked by theorists. Researchers of play tend to agree that the distinguishing characteristics of play include: (1) active engagement, (2) intrinsic motivation, (3) attention to process rather than the ends, (4) nonliteral (symbolic) behavior, and (5) freedom from external rules.[5] Sandra Smidt, an early childhood educationalist, maintained that all play is *purposeful* for the child, in that children "follow their own ideas and their own interests in their own way for their own reasons."[6] Both Sigmund Freud, the founder of psychoanalysis, and developmental psychologist Jean Piaget acknowledged that play is pleasurable.[7] The joy experienced in play compels the child to play.

Theorists have classified different kinds of play — sensori-motor exploration, constructive play, symbolic play, games with rules, rough-and-tumble play. Symbolic play, also known as pretend play, make-believe play, and dramatic play, is the type of play that is the primary focus of this article. It was this type of play that compelled Lev Vygotsky, the psychologist known for his work on social developmental theory and human learning, to write, "In play a child always behaves beyond his average age, above his daily behavior; in play it as though he were a head taller than himself."[8] He believed the symbolic play of children laid the foundation for higher mental functions, such as abstract thought.

Theorists distinguish between spontaneous play and guided play. Spontaneous or free play is initiated by the child and exhibits the characteristics described above. Guided or facilitated play embodies many of the characteristics of free play, however, it is teacher-directed and is used intentionally for educational purposes. It "actively engages children in pleasurable and seemingly spontaneous activities that encourage exploration and learning."[9] At the Warhol, the educators' playful approach to engaging the children with the work of art — such as dancing to music with *Elvis* or creating acetate overlay collages of one's favorite superhero — would be examples of guided play. Back in the kindergarten classroom, the child-initiated superhero fantasy play would be an example of spontaneous play. In their monograph, *A Mandate for Playful Learning in Preschool*, educational researchers Kathy Hirsh-Pasek and her colleagues assert that both approaches to play are essential for children's learning and development.[10]

At the Warhol, I observed the educators' use of play as an effective strategy to actively engage learners and to create a learning environment that was intrinsically motivating. Through supporting children's make-believe play, the educators encouraged the development of identity formation, symbolic thought, and memory-in-action.

Active Engagement

Play actively engages the whole child. Developmental specialists Robert A. McWilliam & Don Bailey define *engagement* as "the amount of time children spend involved with the environment — with the teachers, peers, materials, and [in our case, works of art] — in a way that is appropriate for the children's age, abilities, and surroundings."[11] They maintain that when children are actively engaged with the environment, they "interact with others more, manipulate materials more, and therefore learn more."[12]

Piaget theorized that children construct knowledge through active exploration and engagement with their environment.[13] Vygotsky believed that this active construction of knowledge took place within the social context of others.[14] Philosopher John Dewey saw the child as "spilling over with activities of all kinds," and he viewed education as "taking hold of [the child's] activities, of giving them direction."[15] The Warhol museum educators took hold of the children's play interests (i.e., superheroes) and used their play to give direction to the learning activities during their three hour visit.

As previously defined, play focuses on process rather than outcomes. For the playing child, the process — the action — is what is important. Dewey wrote that play involved "activities performed which are enjoyable, performed for their own sake, and with no end result in mind."[16] He believed that *action* was an essential component of children's learning. He wrote, "The child does not get hold of an idea until he has done it. He acts the idea out before he takes it in."[17]

The activities the Warhol museum educators designed involved *active*, playful, hands-on learning — creating one's own movements to music, playing superheroes in the floating pillow room, silkscreening the capes in the Factory, assembling puzzles, drawing one's favorite foods after learning about Warhol's favorites. Even the open-ended nature of the underpainting activity invited the children to play with the qualities of paint, words, and possibilities, allowing them, as Dewey said, to reproduce experience in imaginative form.[18] Listen to how one child explored the paint: "This paint is really thick. It reminds me of icing. It's like strawberry icing on a birthday cake. I'm going to put my brush in the pink icing and paint the eyes. Oooh, it's gooey. Look, I just gave Andy Warhol strawberry eyes."[19]

Intrinsic Motivation and Flow

Play is intrinsically motivating. Children play because they want to play. The educators can invite, guide and support their play, but the motivation comes from within the child. In the article, "Intrinsic motivation in museums: Why does one want to learn?" psychologists Mihaly Csikszentmihalyi and Hermanson wrote about the *flow* experience in a museum setting.[20] They maintained that flow — a state of optimal pleasure — is more likely to occur when the learner is intrinsically motivated. Since play is intrinsically motivating, children are more likely to be open to learning during play. They wrote, "When playing, children pay attention because they want to, because they find the information interesting and important in its own right."[21]

Although teachers cannot make flow happen, they can create conditions for flow. Finding the "hook" is the first step in engaging the learner.[22] The hook is what intrigues the child, what makes her curious (e.g., creating the cape). Connecting to what is important to the child (e.g., superheroes, make-believe play) makes a "soulful" connection and sustains the child's interests.[23] Engaging the whole child — senses, body, and mind (e.g., playful museum activities) — deepens the child's involvement. Experiencing the pleasure of flow motivates the child to want to continue learning — and return for more.

Identity and Role-play

Play promotes the development and formation of one's personal, social-emotional and cultural identity. Dramatic play, especially the kind that involves dress up and role-playing, allows children to discover "who they could be, who they might be, who they want to be."[24] As they grow in their personal, social and cultural identity, children ask through play, what is it like to be me? What is it like to be somebody else?[25] Through dramatic play, they try on roles of people they know and of people they imagine. Through dramatic play with others — i.e., socio-dramatic play — children discover who they are in relation to other people in their lives.

Pretending allows children to explore how they feel about something. Playing different roles is a way for children to understand how others feel, and socio-dramatic play helps children to understand others' perspectives.[26] This ability to understand another person's point of view is particularly useful in art museums when we invite a group of children to share their ideas about a work of art. We want them to move beyond their own viewpoints to encompass the perspective of others.

Superhero play involves role playing, imagination, and sometimes rough-and-tumble play. Although some adults question its value, early childhood researcher Dorothy Sluss maintains that superhero play has benefits.[27] Cognitively, pretending a piece of fabric is a cape, having objects stand for props, or imagining villains all require symbolic thinking. Just putting on a cape can be enough of a prop for a child to take on all sorts of roles that allow him or her to feel strong and powerful.

Early childhood practitioner, theorist, and storyteller Vivian Gussin Paley reminds us that when children engage in role-playing, they will always act out what concerns them most.[28] Take, for example, the theme of feeling safe, which is a concern shared by many young children. One of the first grade boys who participated in the Warhol kindergarten field trip remembered how frightened he was when he first saw the image of the Wicked Witch. Pretending to be a superhero and attributing supernatural powers to his cape, he told his classmates, "I knew I was safe 'cause I had my cape on." Later that day, inspired by the installation of Warhol's soup boxes, he built his own box fort, creating a safe haven from villains and bad guys.

Symbolic Thought and Imagination

Play fosters the development of symbolic thinking and imagination. Vygotsky believed that the imaginative aspect of play was one of the most powerful learning tools that children used to make sense of their world.[29] In play children move from the reality of the here and now — the world that children experience through their senses — to the imagined world of what might be. They move from the actual to the possible, from the concrete to the abstract, from the 'what is' to answering the question, 'what if,' and acting in ways that suggest 'as if.'[30] When children pretend that a stick can be a light saver or a stone can be a mobile phone, they are using symbols and are beginning to think abstractly — critical to the intellectual development of the child.

Educational theorist Kieran Egan believed that the early childhood curriculum should be developed around imagination and fantasy, particularly because play highlights the passions of children.[31] He recognized that binary opposites frequently occurred in children's play themes, such as good guy/bad guy, danger/rescue, lost/found, the permissible/the forbidden, sense/nonsense. These oppositional tensions that children navigate in their play help them to explore the nature of their physical and social worlds and to better understand who they are within those worlds.

Memory-In-Action

Play helps children make sense of experience. The significance of play in children's learning can continue long after the field trip is over. Cognitive psychologist Jerome Bruner viewed play as a mode of learning and described it as "memory-in-action."[32] "Children play in order to remember and think about events and experiences in their lives that are no longer present and in order to make sense of them."[33] The following play scenario between two girls that occurred after the field trip to the Warhol is a good example of memory-in-action: "We played museum when we got home. We looked around the bedroom and said, 'Hey, let's have a stuffed animal museum.' And we did. And then we decided to have the stuffed animals make art and we pretended the stuffed animals drew all these pictures — but we really drew them — and then we put them up and then we said, 'Hey, let's wear our capes and we can be the teachers and we did."[34]

This is clearly memory-in-action. The children drew on their memory of experiencing a collection, of making and viewing works of art, and of being guided by the museum educators. To this day, the children, as well as their parents, continue to tell me stories about the day of the field trip and beyond.

Conclusion

For educators, play is an essential vehicle for engaging young children in an art museum, and it is an effective strategy for other museums as well. In history museums and historic homes children can pretend to be a person in another place and time — a brother or sister in a one room school house or a craftsperson during Colonial times — related to the exhibition. Science museums invite action on the part of children, from depicting the moving parts of simple machines or showing magnetic attraction through the movement of their bodies. Zoos and botanic gardens can engage children in personifying animal families or representing growing plants.

The superhero play at the Warhol is specific to one museum and one particular group of children at a particular time in their lives. The form and direction of the play we choose to use — whether spontaneous, guided, or both — will be unique to our contexts, the educators' experiences, our collections, and the age and interests of the children.

As educators, we want children to be engaged in learning, and we want the experience to be pleasurable. We also want them to feel safe and comfortable, and we want them return often and eagerly. Through play, we can support their intellectual, emotional, and social development, we can connect to what is important to them in their everyday lives, and we can help them better understand themselves, others, and their world — the real and the possible.

Notes

1. Fred Rogers, *Mister Rogers' Playtime* (Philadelphia: Running Press, 2001), 28.
2. Narrative representation of one child's memory of superhero play.
3. The kindergarten teachers from Falk School included Jill Sarada, Diana Dimitrovski, Jennifer Porter, and Stephanie Weiss. The museum educators from The Warhol included Emily Jaworski, a museum education intern from Penn State University, and Nicole Dezelon, Associate Education Curator: School and Teacher Programs.
4. The following quotations are excerpts from teacher documentation of first grade children's memories of their kindergarten experience at the Warhol.
5. Patricia Monighan-Nourot, Barbara Scales, Judith Van Hoorn, with Millie Almy, *Looking at Children's Play: A Bridge Between Theory and Practice* (New York: Teachers College Press, 1987), 15–19.
6. Sandra Smidt, *Playing to Learn: The Role of Play in the Early Years* (New York: Routledge, 2011), 2. Smidt references Getting Serious About Play — A Review of Children's Play (London: Department for Culture, Media and Sport, 2004).
7. Sigmund Freud, "Creative Writers and Daydreaming," in *The Standard Edition of the Complete Psychological Works of Sigmund Freud* (Vol. IX), ed. James Strachey (London: Hogarth Press, 1959) and Jean Piaget, *Play, Dreams, and Imitation in Childhood* (New York: Norton, 1962).
8. Lev Vygotsky, *Mind in Society* (Cambridge: Harvard University Press, 1978), 102.
9. Kathy Hirsh-Pasek, Roberta Michnick Golinkoff, Laura Berk, and Dorothy Singer, *A Mandate for Playful Learning in Preschool: Presenting the Evidence* (New York: Oxford, 2009), 27.
10. Ibid., *Mandate for Playful Learning.*
11. Quoted in R. A. McWilliam and Amy M. Casey, *Engagement of Every Child in the Preschool Classroom* (Baltimore: Paul H. Brookes, 2008), 4.
12. Ibid., 4.
13. Piaget, *Play, Dreams, and Imitation.*
14. Vygotsky, *Mind in Society.*

15. John Dewey, *The School and Society* (Chicago: University of Chicago Press, 1915/1971).
16. John Dewey, *John Dewey: The Early Works, 1882–1898*, No. 5 (Carbondale: Southern Illinois University Press, 1896/1972), 192–201.
17. John Dewey, "Play," in *A Cyclopedia of Education*, ed. Paul Monroe (New York: Dutton, 1913), 725–727.
18. Dewey, *The school and Society.*
19. Excerpt from teacher documentation of children's conversations during the Warhol museum educators' pre-visit.
20. Mihaly Csikszentmihalyi and Kim Hermanson, "Intrinsic Motivation in Museums: Why Does One Want to Learn?" in John Howard Falk and Lynn Diane Dierking, eds., *Public Institutions for Personal Learning: Establishing a Research Agenda* (Washington DC: American Association of Museums, 1995), 67–77.
21. Ibid., 68.
22. Ibid., 72.
23. Ibid, 73.
24. Louise Boyd Cadwell, *Bringing Learning to Life: The Reggio Approach to Early Childhood Education*, (New York: Teachers College Press, 2002), 189. Cadwell paraphrases the words of Reggio educator, Paola Strozzi.
25. Smidt, *Playing to Learn.*
26. Margaret Donaldson, *Children's Minds* (New York: Norton, 1979).
27. Dorothy Sluss, *Supporting Play: Birth Through Age Eight* (New York: Thomson Delmar Learning, 2005).
28. Vivian Gussin Paley, *A Child's Work: The Importance of Fantasy Play* (Chicago: University of Chicago Press, 2004).
29. Lev Vygotsky, "Play and Its Role in Mental Development of the Child," *Soviet Psychology* 5(3), 6–18.
30. Smidt on Vygotsky, *Playing to Learn*, 11,107.
31. Kieran Egan, *Primary Understanding: Education in Early Childhood* (New York: Routledge, 1988).
32. Jerome Bruner, *Actual Minds, Possible Worlds* (Cambridge: Harvard University Press, 1986).
33. Smidt, *Playing to Learn*, 3.
34. Excerpt from teacher documentation, first graders' memories.

About the Author

Dr. Pamela Krakowski is on the faculty of the University of Pittsburgh in the School of Education. She teaches K-8 art at the university laboratory school, The Falk School. Since 1978, she has also been a part-time museum educator in the Children's Studio at The Carnegie Museum of Art. She is an active member of the Reggio-Pittsburgh Collaborative and is a past president of the Early Childhood Art Educators (ECAE), an issues group within the National Art Education Association.

Thinking Routines

Replicating Classroom Practices within Museum Settings

Rochelle Ibañez Wolberg and Allison Goff

Abstract This article describes thinking routines as tools to guide and support young children's thinking. These learning strategies, developed by Harvard University's Project Zero Classroom, actively engage students in constructing meaning while also understanding their own thinking process. The authors discuss how thinking routines can be used in both classroom and museum settings.

Routines are an expected and integral component of classroom settings. For young children, the repetition of routines contributes to creating a sense of comfort and understanding about the world and how it operates. Routines are particularly significant in early childhood environments, providing the structures in which the youngest students thrive and learn. Within any classroom culture, various routines are used to accomplish specific goals.[1]

Thinking routines from Project Zero offer a defined sequence of actions that lead to making meaning and at the same time help the student gain intellectual control and awareness of the thinking process. For example, children are encouraged to see, think, and wonder when encountering a new object or image. This thinking routine, See/Think/Wonder, establishes specific steps toward gaining new knowledge. When used consistently, it becomes a natural approach that students are able to apply independently.

Project Zero developed thinking routines to strengthen students' thinking abilities and dispositions toward thinking.[2] It involved schools across the world and made use of research from projects such as Innovating with Intelligence and the Artful Thinking Project. Project Zero conducted professional development

Journal of Museum Education, Volume 37, Number 1, Spring 2012, pp. 59–68.

programs to provide teachers with opportunities to revise and modify specific routines to meet their educational needs and goals for students. [3]

Patterns of Thinking

According to Ron Ritchhart, a research associate and principal investigator of the Cultures of Thinking project at Project Zero, routines can help structure classroom conversations. These conversations are purposeful, nurturing students' "patterns of thinking and patterns of behavior."[4]

An important goal of thinking routines is to expose students to the language of thinking.[5] Conversations are extended and the thinking process becomes transparent through the structure and repeated use of the routines. The routines are easy to learn, simple, and goal-directed, and can be used in various contexts to enrich content-specific learning. Certain thinking skills, such as being able to understand different points of view or providing evidence, do not come naturally to young children and must be taught explicitly and strengthened within a learning environment that actively supports the individual student as well as a collective group of children.[6]

Built into each thinking routine is a series of steps that provide teachers with a protocol for facilitating thoughtful discussion amongst students.[7] For example, Think/Puzzle/Explore is useful for examining something new. The routine draws upon students' prior knowledge and encourages them to make connections with what they already know as they inquire about something they may be seeing for the first time. The teacher starts by asking a student, or a group of students, "What do you think you know about this topic or thing?" The teacher follows with the prompt, "What questions or puzzles do you have about it?" The routine ends with the question, "How can you explore this further?" This routine provides time for students to articulate their thoughts and engage in discussions centered on each question. The resulting conversations easily build upon the ones that came before and influence the quality of the next.

Thinking routines can be used to introduce something new, or at the beginning of a lesson or project to generate inquiry. They can be utilized to compare and contrast different works of literature or objects as the teacher moves through a unit. Routines lead toward deeper learning and provide students with strategies for self-directed exploration of concepts and ideas.

Thinking routines are instruments used for the purpose of making students' thinking and learning more visible to themselves, their teachers, and their peers. They contribute to a classroom culture that encourages students to be self-directed learners by giving them the tools to drive their own thinking. This works best when teachers model thinking, allow time for students' thinking, and provide opportunities for students to have purposeful conversations.[8]

Experts in learning theory recognize that thinking routines are tools appropriate for engaging young children in activities that develop and enhance their thinking.[9] Studies have shown that when used within a classroom culture that actively promotes learning and thinking, young children develop positive attitudes toward thinking. One qualitative study, conducted with children between the ages of 3 and 6, concludes that utilizing thinking routines within a classroom culture that supports quality interactions helps to make students more sensitive to situations that call for specific thinking skills.[10] Children are more alert and readily able to participate in activities, such as those that encourage further inquiry and exploration.

Thinking routines are successfully being used in formal learning environments. But are thinking routines useful in informal learning environments? Are they appropriate for engaging students with art and artifacts in museums? Will they serve the educational goals of museums and facilitate open-ended inquiry and deeper conversations that delve beneath the surface? Our experience suggests that when utilized strategically by museum educators, thinking routines can further enhance a child's learning even within the limited time frame of a museum visit. The learning is enhanced further when similar patterns of thinking are used to engage students in museums and classrooms. When reinforced and supported across a variety of settings learning has greater impact on promoting understanding, especially for the young child.

Examining Developmental Principles That Inform Educational Practices

Providing high-quality education for young children is receiving significant attention and investment in today's world, particularly in relation to standards that influence educational practices.[11] As such, educators working in early childhood settings must balance curricular expectations with developmentally appropriate practices. Three interconnected principles serve as the theoretical framework behind the utilization of thinking routines.

According to the first principle, the experience of constructing meaning involves a variety of social contexts and experiences. Developmental psychologist, Jean Piaget, believed that children have the capacity to construct meaning out of interactions with their environment.[12] Graham Nuthall, a pioneer researcher whose research focused on the relationships between teachers and students, makes similar observations and posits, "What creates or shapes learning is a sequence of events or experiences, each one building on the effects of the previous one."[13]

The second principle addresses language acquisition. Progress in language attainment carries over into other areas of the young child's life. Most notably, language directly affects cognitive development. Psychologist Lev Vygotsky "viewed language as the main 'engine' of intellectual growth."[14] When teachers give young children a common language of thinking, the children receive tools they can use, adapt, and practice in other areas of their life.

The third principle emphasizes the fundamental role of social interaction in promoting understanding. Project Zero's David Perkins and Ron Ritchhart assert that the "classroom culture . . . can support or undermine the rhythm of thoughtful learning."[15] One can easily insert "museum culture" into that statement, as an environment that can set the expectation and provide ways for children to learn and create meaning through their engagement with art and cultural artifacts.

There is a legitimate argument for replicating the classroom "culture of thinking" into museums, which provide a distinct informal learning experience.[16] "Thinking" encompasses a range of cognitive abilities that include making comparisons, reasoning, analyzing, deducing, and reflecting, skills that are relevant regardless of the learning environment. A child who is exposed to different types of thinking in the museum becomes more aware of new and meaningful ways for interacting with art and artifacts. Effective learning strategies are useful in multiple settings.

Guiding a Conversation with See/Think/Wonder

What exactly occurs during a thinking routine? What follows is a description of a See/Think/Wonder routine with preschool students.

Palm Beach Day Academy teachers are diligent in their efforts to establish thoughtful learning environments within their classrooms. The utilization of thinking routines is an example of how teachers elicit and support thinking moves (e.g., observing, getting at the essence of something, looking through the lens of multiple perspectives) in their students.

The See/Think/Wonder (STW) routine provides a straightforward pattern of discourse that encourages students to be curious and creative in their thinking. It is grounded in "careful observations and thoughtful interpretations" revolving around an image or artifact.[17] Students describe initial observations, share why they think an object or image looks the way it does, and then ponder about any other aspects that remain unclear to them. It is one of the most popular routines because it is straightforward, fairly easy to implement, and naturally leads to open-ended inquiry. [18]

Jessica Laliberte, a primary teacher working with preschool students, incorporated STW during a lesson on camouflage. Laliberte presented her young pupils with a picture of a tiger lurking behind some foliage in a jungle setting. This image served as the provocation toward further inquiry. When Laliberte asked, What do you SEE?" children replied, "I see orange and black stripes," "I can see lots of leaves and trees," and "I see the tiger is in the jungle." As the children shared their thoughts, Laliberte recorded the student responses on the white board. This action captured the children's thoughts in a concrete format and made their thinking visible.

Laliberte followed up with the question, "What do you THINK about what you see?" At this point in the discussion, students needed to provide further insight into their initial observations. One child stated, "I think the tiger is hunting for food." A young girl, after much thought stated aloud, "I think he's [the tiger] looking at something he's hunting for." After jotting down a number of responses, Laliberte modeled for her class what wondering about something might look like. She placed her index finger to her temple, scratched, and sighed aloud "Hmm, I wonder" before asking the children to share anything in the picture that still puzzled them.

At this prompt, one little girl asked, "I WONDER if the tiger has babies?" Another student responded loudly with the statement, "I wonder if the tiger is looking at a predator." In modeling for the students what puzzling over something may look like, Laliberte opened a doorway for them to share some very original and advanced thoughts. There were no right or wrong answers, simply opportunities for the children to share their thoughts within an evolving conversation.

It is essential to nurture within young children the inclination to use their thinking skills in various situations. A teacher does this through modeling what thinking looks like for their young students. When children see how their teacher thinks, questions, and wonders aloud, it affects how they view their own thinking. Young children become more capable of making jumps and leaps in the thinking process when they see it being modeled and practice these skills in different contexts. A museum provides a different setting for practicing the skills, and museums' art and artifacts, often not part of the children's daily life experiences, can excite, stimulate, and inspire.

Young Children and Thinking in the Museum

Museums often find young audiences challenging, especially when they can't allow children to touch collection items. The Henry Morrison Flagler Museum's education department has successfully used the "thinking" component of Think/Puzzle/Explore to engage young children within the constraints of museum rules.

The Mission of the Henry Morrison Flagler Museum is to preserve, research, and interpret Whitehall, its associated collections, and materials related to the life of Henry Morrison Flagler, as unique and important elements of Florida's history and America's Gilded Age. The overall goal of the museum's education department is to provide programming that serves to engage, inspire, and educate all audiences. Much of the museum's programming comes in the form of traditional interpretive tours, but when deeper, concise learning is the desired outcome and when time is limited, museum educators turn to the "thinking" strategy to provide information while energizing students to be expressive with their thoughts.

The "thinking" component of Think/Puzzle/Explore is similar to Abigail Housen and Philip Yenawine's Visual Thinking Strategies (VTS).[19] Thinking routines lead to open-ended inquiry by asking young visitors to first react to a visual cue then go beyond the cue and make an inference or formulate an idea based on reason. The ability to extend the process in Think/Puzzle/Explore is seen as a way to encourage young visitors to make personal connections and process information within the experience of viewing, learning and enjoying an object or concept. The use of thinking routines fosters more creative and dynamic thinking and ultimately a more effective understanding of history for the young visitor.

The education department seeks to incorporate formal learning strategies into all of its school-age programming, whether it is in the form of arts integration into core subjects such as math and science, incorporating K-12 curriculum standards in language arts and social studies lesson plans, or adopting classroom management techniques on an individualized level during tours and outreach programming.

One goal of the education department's school-based programming is to become an extension of the traditional classroom; to be a resource for teachers and students where learning continues and connections are made. Without integrating the teaching methods already in place in a young visitor's learning routine, a museum tour or program is an esoteric experience outside of the classroom and often results in little or no transference beyond that isolated experience.

Museums are a unique learning environment in comparison to classrooms. With access to historic documents, images, and collection items, young visitors are not only exposed to primary resources as learning tools but also to interpretations of the past, guided connections to history. By adopting the existing methods of partner schools and individual classrooms, museum educators are able to disseminate interpretive material without the additional challenge of introducing new teaching approaches. When this happens, the Flagler Museum functions as an extension of classroom learning and exposure to the museum's collection and interpretive material is efficient and effective.

In one example, museum educators use thinking routines with first grade students. The main goals of the lesson of focus are to introduce the concepts of community development and Henry Flagler's influence on the development of Florida. Thinking routines help educators gauge the students' prior knowledge and the use of props and role-play provide tactile exposure to the Gilded Age. After introducing core concepts, the museum educator initiates a prop-based tableau that combines interpretive delivery and the thinking routines "What do you see/What makes you say that?"

A student volunteer represents the settlers of the Lake Worth region using a straw hat as a prop symbolic of the pioneer community. The educator poses a series of questions asking students to describe a typical day or the most challenging part of a job. The educator probes, "What makes you say that? Knowing what you do about the history we have discussed so far, how do you think farming has changed since 1873?"

While young visitors to the Flagler Museum are exposed to art through the building's architecture and the cultural artifacts found within, Whitehall is a historic house museum. Interpretation and programming focuses on history; the lives of the people who lived at Whitehall and their significance in history, rather than on the collection objects themselves. While VTS is effective, especially when objects are visually accessible, the museum's use of thinking routines expands the students' visual thinking and encourages them to use it in the exploration of even the more abstract concepts. Using thinking routines, the information gathered by a student comes not just from visual cues within the collection, but also from thoughtful inference, reason, and deduction.

As a result, the museum educator receives immediate feedback as to whether students understand the main concepts of the lesson. When students respond with thoughtful answers, gathered from image or object inference, that interaction confirms for the educator that it is appropriate to continue to add content to the learning platform.

Museum experiences are about looking, reflecting, and making meaning from the objects and interpretation presented. Strategies such as thinking routines engage students in this same process of making meaning but offer a more structured routine where students also begin to understand the process of thinking and its application to learning.

The Classroom and Museum Collaboration: A Bridge to Strengthening Thinking

Museum educators have access to a variety of educational materials that can enhance the thinking skills that classroom teachers encourage and promote. Educational partnerships between schools and museums can strengthen student learning, or in general, enrich the learning experience of young children.

A collaborative model using thinking routines is in place between Palm Beach Day Academy, the Flagler Museum, and the Morikami Museum. This year, both museums will partner with the school on a new curricular project for first grade students focusing on the concept of communities. Through archived photographs and cultural artifacts that will be used in a series of presentations conducted by museum educators, the children will learn about the unique communities that existed in early South Florida history. The children will also learn and recognize the role that museums play in preserving the legacy and history of communities. It is not only the content introduced through the museum experiences that is important in this collaboration, but the reinforcement of ways of thinking that will cut across the boundaries of school and museum.

This type or partnership cannot happen within a vacuum. It is a social endeavor that requires diverse educators working together across their spheres of expertise and choosing strategies that are relevant and practical to each setting. Thinking routines are simple, yet effective techniques that can enhance students' experiences and understanding because they are adaptable for various contexts.

Various thinking routines, such as See/Think/Wonder and Circle of Viewpoints, in which students pick a point of view and speak from it, will be used specifically to give the children an opportunity to glean information from what they see, build connections, make associations, and form interpretations. The children will explore new ideas through introductory sessions at school as well as field trips to the respective museums. Collectively, these experiences will create a narrative of the students' learning and thinking about communities.

Conclusion

A collaborative model in which school and museum educators are both utilizing an effective learning strategy, such as thinking routines, strengthens and supports student learning and thinking. The opportunity to use strategies and develop skills within multiple contexts nurtures the learning process and makes the entire experience more personal and relevant to the children and educators. The purpose of thinking routines — supporting the disposition toward thinking — is a common goal for both formal and informal learning environments. Research by Harvard's Project Zero documents the success of thinking routines for supporting student learning in the classroom setting. These same strategies can be utilized in museums, independently or in partnership with a traditional educational entity, such as a school. The routines, because they are simple, explicit, easy to learn, and goal-directed, offer museum educators another strategy for creating powerful learning experiences for visitors, in particular, young children.

Notes

1. Angela Salmon, "Engaging Young Children in Thinking Routines." *Childhood Education* 86 (2010): 132–137; Ron Ritchhart and others, "Thinking Routines: Establishing Patterns of Thinking in the Classroom" (paper prepared at the AERA Conference, San Francisco, 2006).
2. "Visible Thinking," Project Zero, http://www.pz.harvard.edu/research/VisThink.htm (accessed September 2010).
3. Ritchhart and others, "Thinking Routines."
4. Ron Ritchhart, *Intellectual Character: What It Is, Why It Matters, and How To Get It* (San Francisco: Jossey-Bass, 2002), 229.
5. Shari Tishman, David Perkins, and Eileen Jay, *The Thinking Classroom: Learning and Teaching in a Culture of Thinking* (Boston: Allyn and Bacon, 1995).
6. Carol Copple and Sue Bredekamp, eds. *Developmentally Appropriate Practice in Early Childhood Programs Serving Children from Birth through Age 8*, 3rd ed. (Washington, DC: National Association for the Education of Young Children, 2009); Angela K. Salmon, "Promoting a Culture of Thinking in the Young Child," *Early Childhood Education Journal* 35 (2008): 457–461.
7. Angela K. Salmon, "Tools to Enhance Young Children's Thinking," *Young Children* (2010): 26–31; Ritchhart and others, "Thinking Routines."
8. Ritchhart, *Intellectual Character.*
9. Salmon, "Engaging Young Children in Thinking Routines."; Salmon, "Tools to Enhance Young Children's Thinking."
10. Salmon, "Promoting a Culture of Thinking in the Young Child."
11. NAEYC & NAECS/SDE (National Association for the Education of Young Children and National Association of Early Childhood Specialists in State Departments of Education), "Early Learning Standards: Creating the Conditions for Success," Joint position statement. (2002), http://www.naeyc.org/files/naeyc/file/positions/position_statement.pdf (accessed March 15, 2011): 1.
12. Jean Piaget, *The Origins of Intelligence in Children* (New York: International Universities Press, 1952).

13. Graham Nuthall, "The Cultural Myths and the Realities of Teaching and Learning" (address presented at The Jean Herbison Lecture, December 2001), Educational Leaders, http://www.educationalleaders.govt.nz/Pedagogy-and-assessment/Evidence-based-leadership/Data-gathering-and-analysis/The-cultural-myths-and-realities-of-teaching-and-learning (accessed January 6, 2011): 10.
14. John Houtz, *The Skills of Teaching: Using Educational Objectives and Assessing Learner Knowledge and Learning Styles* (John Houtz, 2000), 53.
15. Ron Ritchhart and David Perkins, "Making Thinking Visible," *Educational Leadership* 65 (2008): 57–61.
16. Ron Ritchhart, "Cultivating a Culture of Thinking in Museums," *Journal of Museum Education* 32 (2007).
17. "See/Think/Wonder Routine," Visible Thinking, Harvard Project Zero, http://www.pz.harvard.edu/vt/visibleThinking_html_files/03_ThinkingRoutines/03c_Core_routines/SeeThinkWonder/SeeThinkWonder_Routine.html (accessed September 13, 2010).
18. Ritchhart, "Thinking Routines."
19. Abigail Housen and Philip Yenawine, "Understanding the Basics: Visual Understanding in Education," http://www.vue.org/download.html (accessed October 2009).

About the Authors

Rochelle Ibañez Wolberg is the learning specialist and Coordinator of Support Services at Palm Beach Day Academy. She works directly with students, consults with parents, and mentors faculty in the Visible Thinking approach and use of Thinking Routines. She presented a picture of practice, "A Learning Odyssey with 1,000 Paper Cranes," during the 2011 Making Learning Visible Conference, hosted by Florida International University and senior researchers from Project Zero, which highlighted the work of second graders during a yearlong study of peace and symbolism. She holds graduate degrees in Educational Psychology and School Psychology from Fordham University.

Allison Goff is the Education Director at the Flagler Museum in Palm Beach, Florida, where she oversees the development and facilitation of educational programming and interpretation. Ms. Goff was formerly a high school teacher and has a professional background in literacy and ELL instruction through AmeriCorps. She holds a Bachelors of Science in Interdisciplinary Studies of Social Science and Anthropology from Michigan State University.

Collaboration is the Key

Artists, Museums, and Children

Melina Mallos

Abstract Often considered places of solemn contemplation, quiet inspiration and personal reflection, art museums seem among the most reluctant to embrace early childhood audiences. Melina Mallos discusses action research at the Queensland Art Gallery | Gallery of Modern Art, Australia, as a means of gaining new insight into children's learning and ways to embrace this audience. The article focuses on three artist projects to describe the collaboration between artists and museums necessary to create memorable encounters with contemporary art for young audiences.

Young children are becoming a more significant audience in today's museums, which requires thoughtful consideration about how to best engage this unique group. Across Australia, museums offer programs for families and children with the goal of securing lifelong relationships. Educational consultants in Australia have noted that, "to build and sustain the relationships, some museums have adopted child-centered policies and programs when designing and interpreting their collections for early childhood audiences."[1]

Over the past decade or so, Australian art museums have increasingly focused on creating more stimulating and interactive opportunities for children. Best practice for engaging these young audiences involves combining active and reflective learning opportunities to educate, engage and entertain young visitors.[2] Many museums are offering opportunities for handling objects, dramatic play, experimentation, construction and art-making. Research indicates that in order for children to purposefully interact and engage with art in museums, the following elements are essential:

Journal of Museum Education, Volume 37, Number 1, Spring 2012, pp. 69–80.

- a sensory-rich environment
- exhibits which build upon children's interests, prior knowledge and experiences
- a focus on stimulating children's curiosity, interest and learning
- opportunities for personal meaning making
- shared interaction and responsive dialogues with adults and peers
- opportunities to explore, play and engage in self-directed activity.[3]

Davis and Garner outline three strategies useful for cultivating children's encounters with art.[4] The experiential window, or "hands-on" approach, invites children to touch, manipulate or respond using bodily movements; the narrative window allows children to experience an object through the medium of story; and the aesthetic window focuses on having children describe the visual and aesthetic qualities of the object encountered.

Visitors to art museums are increasingly seeing forms of collaboration in the making of contemporary art — from artistic partnerships and collectives, to audience participation, community involvement and social engagement. This relatively recent shift towards collaborative aspects of art-making draws further attention to the importance of inclusiveness; that people contribute meaning and relevance to art.[5] Kate Ryan and Donna McColm from the Queensland Art Gallery | Gallery of Modern Art explain that it is this expanding interest in collaboration by artists, which in turn has informed art museum practice, that has provided an ideal climate for engaging children in contemporary art.[6]

This article will discuss how artist projects created especially for children enable these young visitors to take part in the thinking and making processes of contemporary artists. Children's active participation in such experiences helps build an understanding and knowledge of today's contemporary art and the diversity of cultures from which it springs. The three artist projects described are interactive, thought-provoking and innovative — like much of today's successful contemporary art — and, most importantly, fun.[7]

Building relationships with Young Children

For many children and families, the Queensland Art Gallery and its second site, the Gallery of Modern Art, is seen as a place of learning, fun and playfulness. The organization is situated in the cultural precinct of Brisbane across two separate buildings, which were Australia's most visited museums last year, attracting 1.8 million people. On the international circuit, the museums were ranked 18th in the world.[8]

Since 1998, the Queensland Art Gallery has engaged in innovative exhibition and education programming for young audiences. Underpinning its philosophy is the idea that children could, and should, be recognized and fostered as "legitimate, receptive viewers of contemporary art."[9] One of the driving forces behind the establishment of its second site, the Gallery of Modern Art, in 2006, was the provision of the Children's Art Centre, a dedicated space for children and families. The gallery's Director, Tony Ellwood, stressed how this space highlighted to the Queensland community the high value the organization placed on facilitating young children's engagement with art.

The Children's Art Centre has been integral to the increase in audience engagement at the museum. Although a permanent physical space in the Gallery of Modern Art building, the Centre also presents programs across both galleries.

Central to the gallery's children's programs are specially commissioned artist projects for children from 0 to 12 years to engage with; artists are invited to develop an interactive experience within the Children's Art Centre itself or dedicated exhibition spaces. These are usually hands-on activities that encourage children to make connections to ideas or materials with which the artists work in their practice. At the same time, this engagement serves as a link to the artists' work on display at the gallery, enhancing the accessibility of art to young audiences. To date, gallery staff members have collaborated with more than 100 Australian and international contemporary artists to develop exhibitions, projects, installations and workshops for children and families.

Early Experimentation: Kids' APT

The gallery's collaborative endeavors in children's programs began with the *First Asia Pacific Triennial of Contemporary Art* (APT1). Held from 17 September to 5 December 1993, it was the first project of its kind in the world to focus on the contemporary art of Asia and the Pacific. The ongoing series of exhibitions and forums aim to initiate dialogue on the art of this important geo-political region. In 1999, for the third triennial in the series, the gallery openly acknowledged children as a key audience for this international contemporary art event. The inaugural Kids' APT program exemplifies the collaboration between artist, museum and children. Several major international artists were commissioned to work with the gallery's education staff to develop activities that would serve to enhance children's understanding of their artworks in the exhibition.

Cai Guo-Qiang: *Blue Dragon and Bridge Crossing* 1999

When visiting the gallery in 2000, 11-year-old Sally pointed excitedly to the Watermall and said, 'That's where the bridge was!'[10] She was referring to Chinese artist Cai Guo-Qiang's *Blue Dragon and Bridge Crossing* 1999 — a graceful 30-metre-long bamboo construction which the artist built over the main pool of the Watermall for the *Third Asia Pacific Triennial of Contemporary Art* in 1999. Part-way through crossing the bridge, visitors were sprayed with a fine mist. While visitors could begin the crossing from either end, the bridge was not wide enough for two people to pass each other. The work explored ideas of compromise and decision-making.

Sally's moment of recognition is a crucial factor in a set of creative learning strategies to help children make connections between their experience, their growing awareness of art practices, and their familiarity with the gallery's spaces. The combination of the initial interaction with an exhibit in-gallery and the subsequent opportunity to act on and assimilate the experience is seen as an opportunity to create a more lasting outcome.

Some of the most successful projects have involved artists conceiving of interactive spaces that encourage children's own creativity. For Kids' APT, Cai Guo-Qiang developed an activity in which children were invited to design and construct a bridge using fine pieces of cane and masking tape. The artist made 76 line drawings of various bridges from around the world and attached them to a sunlit glass wall next to his work. In front of the wall was a long workbench at which children could sit to assemble the model bridges through the day. Children could be seen engrossed in the process of engineering and fabricating their individual creations.

What did this artist project teach gallery staff? Making an artist's work accessible to children is necessary to link the artist, their work and the children's own art-making. Having the artist's work directly adjacent to the activity space stimulated questions and conversation and encouraged children to revisit the exhibition to examine the art work more closely.

Visitors nominated Kids' APT as one of the most appealing elements of the 1999 Asia Pacific Triennial, with senior gallery staff commenting that "What the first Kids' APT proved beyond doubt is that children are naturally attracted to contemporary art — to its abstractions, diversity, scale and experimentation."[11] Since then, the gallery's philosophy of working directly with contemporary artists to develop projects for children has attracted more than one million visitors to children's exhibitions and programs.

The children's experiences facilitated through Kids' APT influenced the gallery's approach to working with artists when designing future children's programs in a museum context. Incorporating the artist's perspective allows for encounters and engagements that are social, artistic and aesthetic. The involvement of artists in the design of Kids' APT programs has been paramount in presenting a program of integrity, providing children with new ideas and approaches to making art. Every project is different, and every artist approaches the challenge of creating for and communicating with kids in a unique way.[12] The programs rely on a partnership between the artist and audience. Visitors become, in effect, art-makers; they respond to the artist's invitation to participate and contribute to the creative process.[13]

Few galleries, anywhere, have devoted more thought and energy to shaping a program that entrances children. And few, surely, come close to achieving this level of response. The Kids' APT's true brilliance is that at no point does it talk down to children, or even consider that many of the concepts are difficult.[14]

Research Background

The first research project focusing on children's learning at the Queensland Art Gallery was "Share the Joy," conducted by Dr. Barbara Piscitelli in the late 1980s. Since that time, experimentation and direct observation has informed ideas about children's programs at the gallery. The research that organizational staff conducted over several decades was critical to development of the gallery's children's programs, beginning with small-scale studies that resulted in a sustained partnership with the Queensland University of Technology (QUT). The gallery was one of four museums in the QUT Museums Collaborative, which "aimed to collaboratively develop, foster and enrich young visitors' museum experiences through research, training and staff development."[15]

This collaboration culminated in the recognition of the need for the establishment of a dedicated space to provide ongoing opportunities, all year round, for families to partake in — to become the Children's Art Centre at the gallery's second site from 2006. However, prior to the opening of the Children's Art Centre, the APT exhibitions continued to provide opportunities for both gallery staff and artists to explore the potential of engaging in meaningful ways with children.

Yayoi Kusama: *The Obliteration Room* 2002

Children are an important audience valued by the gallery, and this is reflected, through its commitment to enlisting senior international artists to realize projects for children. One of the most successful projects was Japanese artist Yayoi Kusama's *The Obliteration Room* 2002 developed for Kids' APT 2002. The artist's instruction for her children's installation were quite specific: create a room similar to an Australian living room, furnish it with typical household items, paint the room and all its contents white, give children colored dots of various sizes, and invite them to "obliterate" the whole environment by sticking dots everywhere (including, if they wished, on themselves).

Kusama creates large-scale works that play with the way we see ourselves and the environment. She likes us to see how she views the world, through a screen of dots. Kusama also likes to experiment with how the audience views themselves and each other in her dot environments. The viewer is incorporated into her art works, their physical appearance transformed to match the surroundings. In this way, the viewer is participating in, and becomes part of, the artwork. *The Obliteration Room* 2002 proved to be popular, and seemed to have the ideal combination of ingredients for a contemporary art installation for children. It was engaging and fun for kids while remaining true to the artist's own practice.

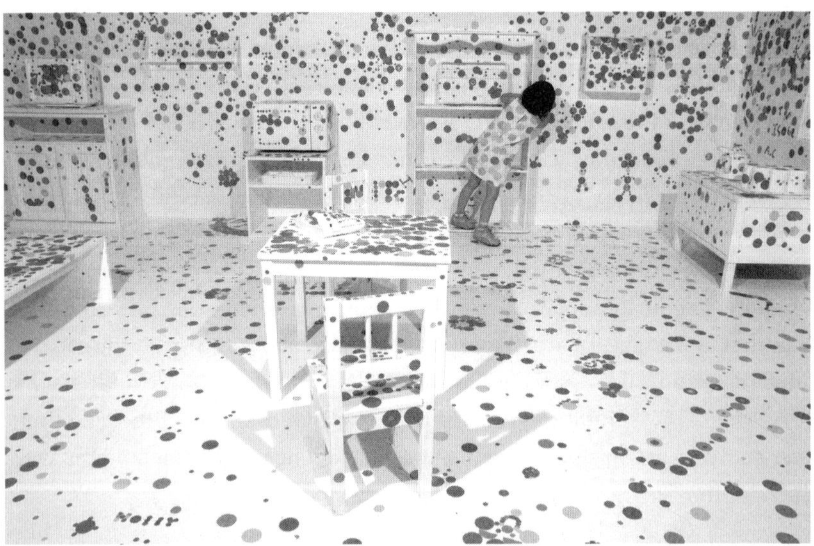

Yayoi Kusama's *The Obliteration Room* 2002, commissioned for Kids' APT. Photograph: Natasha Harth

During 2003–04, following on from the success of the children's programs of APT 2002, a series of visitor studies were conducted at the Queensland Art Gallery by a team of researchers from the gallery and QUT, revealing the need to ensure that interactive programs were sensitive to young children's development, knowledge, prior experiences and interests.[16] The research undertaken focused on particular segments of the child and family audience, and was used to inform the development of policies and programs. Financial and operational plans for visitor services as well as records of environmental designs, front-end planning and administrative decisions relating to programs for young children were implemented.

Over the first few years of formal research, researchers tracked and observed audience behavior. Staff pre-tested, sought advice, and tested and revised designs to develop interactive programs for young audiences. These days, school trials, parent surveys, on-site evaluations and children's interviews form the basis of the gallery's ongoing research agenda. In addition, museum staff conduct video interviews with artists, children, parents and teachers, which is proving to be an incredibly useful tool for documenting and evaluating the learning outcomes of children's programs.

Planning, Design and Implementation: A Collaborative Process

The Queensland Art Gallery example of children's programs begins with the work of an artist and a conceptual plan by curators, exhibition designers and educators for the purpose of connecting children to ideas and aesthetics related to art. As exhibits are designed, feedback from children in the gallery and others taking part in trials at local schools informs the curatorial process and the final design for the program. The process also takes into consideration the style of learning associated with children, emphasizing the need to stimulate learning through experimentation, investigation and discovery. It is this collaborative process that begins with the artist, and is ultimately shaped by the ideas of children and museum professionals. Cultivating community participation and sense of ownership are imperative.

Gablik in *The Reenchantment of Art* claims that artists are beginning to see their role with a different sense of purpose, with "a new emphasis on community and environment rather than on individual achievement and accomplishment."[17] She espouses "the emergence of a more participatory, socially interactive framework for art."[18] Indeed, the strength of the Kids' APT projects lies in the ideas of the artists and the working relationship with gallery staff. Curators, exhibition and graphic designers, workshop staff and educators meet regularly and collaboratively realize the projects, whilst in constant communication with the artists.

Experimenting with ideas and evaluating the durability of design features is undertaken at the testing phase. The challenge is to find authentic ways for children to connect to the artist's use of materials, ideas and techniques. Each staff member brings different areas of expertise, ways of seeing and working and multiple perspectives, which allow programs to be successfully executed. With each new artist collaboration, staff seeks to discover different ways for children to access contemporary art. Another wonderful outcome is that the projects enable the artists to explore aspects of their practice in new, and often unexpected, ways.[19] The Kids' APT projects promote this type of learning, and illustrate the ways children actively recall and remember their encounters with interactive projects at the gallery.

Alfredo & Isabel Aquilizan: *In-flight (Project: Another Country)* 2009

Gallery staff have observed that children are able to readily recall exhibit components that they directly participated in, or make a connection between a children's project and the exhibiting artists' work.[20] *In-flight (Project: Another Country)* 2009 is a great example of this. Husband-and-wife team Isabel and Alfredo Aquilizan invited the local Brisbane community to make a small airplane from recycled material and add it to the larger constellation of a huge airplane; as such, the work literally took shape through the contribution of individuals to the collective whole. Central to Alfredo and Isabel Aquilizan's philosophy of involving the community in their art is that ". . . kids and adults alike have the opportunity to experience a participatory work, and artwork that grows with the contribution of everybody."[21]

In-flight (Project: Another Country) 2009 is part of an ongoing series which addresses the artists' experience of migration. The Aquilizans' recent settlement in Australia from the Philippines and the necessity to construct a new home — not only a physical space, but also a different kind of being-at-home in this land of near-strangers — provided them with an opportunity and even more intense energy to carry out their creative practice.[22] The complete experience, from the decisions to emigrate, to the journey itself, to finding a footing in a new country, is captured in the exchanges that take place within this important project. Speaking of the planes made from recycled and found objects by visitors, Lynne Seear, then Deputy Director of the gallery, remarked, "So magical are these

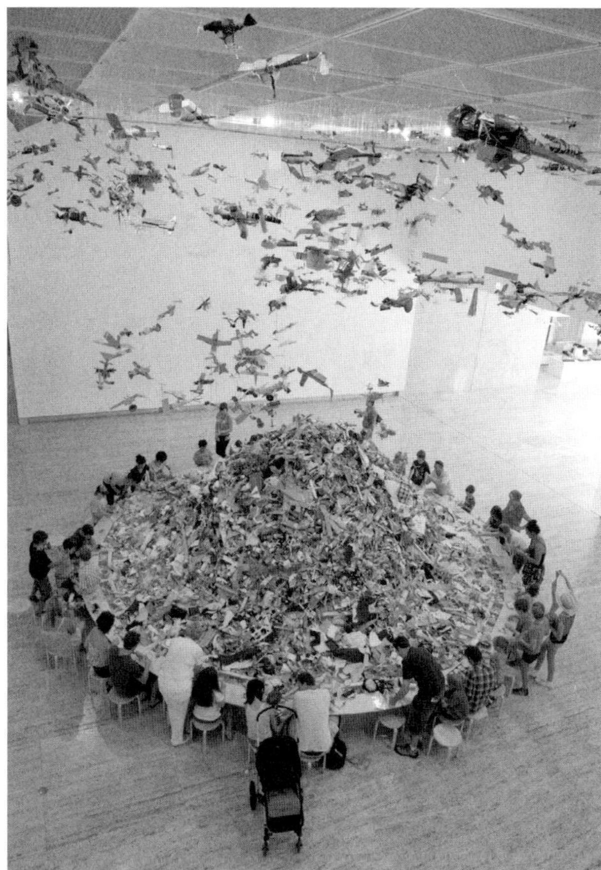

In-flight (Project: Another Country) 2009, a site-specific work for The 6th Asia Pacific Triennial of Contemporary Art. Photograph: Ray Fulton

objects, so imbued with human hope and talent that it is possible to believe in their actual capacity for flight."[23]

As they made their planes, families, schools, students and children contemplated ideas about travel, flight and migration. Each participant, by making and adding a plane to the collective, contributed to a group work made by their local community. Communities working together was one of the messages the project highlighted in providing an appropriate environment and atmosphere for collaborative art-making experiences. The project was in keeping with the notions of flexibility, collaboration and making do, embedded in the artists' practice. More than 65 schools across Queensland took part in making airplanes for the installation, contributing more than 6500 planes.[24]

Because Alfredo and Isabel Aquilizan's *In-flight* so seamlessly navigates and connects the Asia Pacific Triennial exhibition with Kids' APT, it acts as model for

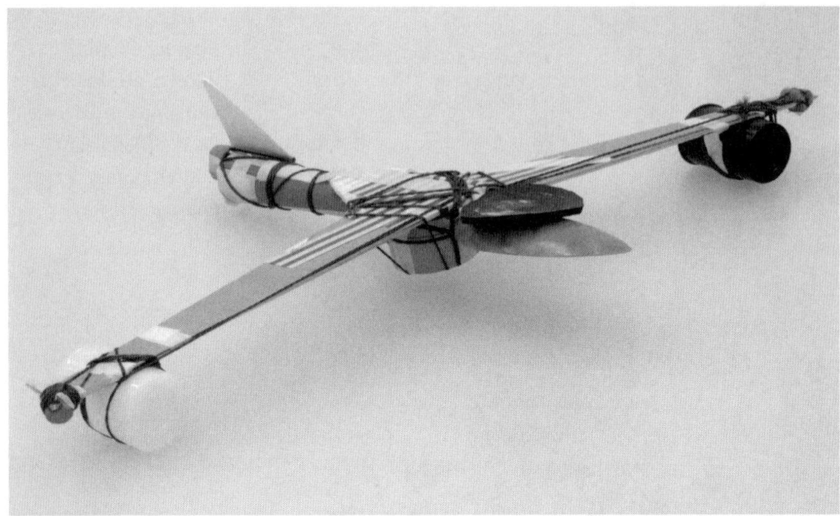

A plane the Aquilizans created out of recycled materials for their installation, *In-flight (Project: Another Country)* 2009. Photograph: Natasha Harth

future Kids' APT projects. This unique project is so obviously successful in engaging minds and bodies in the act of creation, while, at the same time, strengthening social bonds.[25]

The Future of Children's Museum Programs

For all their diversity, the gallery's Children's Art Centre projects share the common aim of building, for each young visitor, a storehouse of experiences and memories that will contribute over time to opening his or her mind to creativity, knowledge and the richness of human endeavor and culture in all its forms.[26]

Museums are dynamic learning places for children and adults to share their thoughts, feelings, observations and understanding of ideas contained in exhibits and objects. Young children learn as they watch and listen to others, work collaboratively to solve problems, discuss their ideas and ask questions. Effective exhibit design accommodates multiple users in multigenerational learning circles, promoting discussion and providing opportunities for group work. Conversation, questioning and opportunities for reflection are essential in programming for young children in all types of museums.

A strong research framework, a collaborative approach to planning and design, and the unique perspective of an artist are essential features for successful children's programs. By combining artists' ideas and perspectives on art-making for children with the functional and aesthetically vibrant spaces designed by in-house museum staff, museums and galleries are contributing towards the development of dynamic children's programming into the future.

Notes

1. Barbara Piscitelli, Katrina Weier and Michele Everett, "Museums and Young Children: Partners in Learning about the World", in *Children, Meaning-Making and the Arts*, ed. Susan Wright (Pearson Education Australia, 2003), 167.
2. Barbara Piscitelli, "Designing Galleries with Children in Mind", in *Exploring Culture and Community for the 21st Century*, ed. B. Henson (Ipswich: Global Arts Link, 1999), 99–101.
3. M.K. Judd and J.B. Kracht, "The World at their Fingertips: Children in Museums", in *Learning Opportunities Beyond the School*, eds. B. Hatcher and S.S. Beck (Washington, DC: Association for Childhood Education International, 1997), 21–26.
4. J. Davis and H. Gardner, "The Arts and Early Childhood Education: A Cognitive Developmental Portrait of the Young Child as Artist", in *Handbook of Research on the Education of Young Children*, ed. B. Spodek (New York: Macmillan, 1993). 191–206.
5. Charles Green, *The Third Hand: Collaboration in Art from Conceptualism to Post-Modernism* (Sydney: University of New South Wales Press, 2011), 40.
6. Kate Ryan and Donna McColm, "Collaboration and Contemporary Art Projects," in *Contemporary Art for Contemporary Kids* (Sherman Contemporary Art Foundation and Queensland Art Gallery, 2010), 41.
7. Tony Ellwood, "A Note from Tony Ellwood," in *Contemporary Art for Contemporary Kids* (Sherman Contemporary Art Foundation and Queensland Art Gallery, 2010), 44.
8. "Exhibition and museum attendance figures 2010", *The Art Newspaper*, no. 223, April, 2011, www.theartnewspaper.com/attfig/attfig10.pdf (accessed June 11, 2011).
9. Andrew Clark, "Contemporary Art for Contemporary Kids: In the Now and for the Future," in *Contemporary Art for Contemporary Kids* (Sherman Contemporary Art Foundation and Queensland Art Gallery, 2010), 36.
10. Kate Ravenswood and Melina Mallos, "Explore, Discover, Interact: Let's Play," *Artlines: Art and People* 3 (2005), 24.
11. Lynne Seear and Andrew Clark, "Contemporary art for contemporary kids," *Artlines: Art and People* 3 (2005), 20.
12. Andrew Clark, "Contemporary Art for Contemporary Kids: In the Now and for the Future," in *Contemporary Art for Contemporary Kids* (Sherman Contemporary Art Foundation and Queensland Art Gallery, 2010), 38.
13. Gene Sherman, "Paths to Learning' Contemporary art for contemporary kids," in *Contemporary Art for Contemporary Kids* (Sherman Contemporary Art Foundation and Queensland Art Gallery, 2010), 35.
14. Bob Hart, "Kids' APT — A Collaboration: Sponsorship in Review," *Tim Fairfax Family Foundation* (Queensland Art Gallery, 2009), 13.
15. QUT Museums Learning Collaborative, "The QUT Museum Learning Collaborative: Young Children's Interactive and Informal Learning in Museums", http://www.ed.qut.edu.au/ec/museums/col.html (accessed May 14, 2002), 2.
16. QUT Museums Learning Collaborative, "The QUT Museum Learning Collaborative: Young Children's Interactive and Informal Learning in Museums", http://www.ed.qut.edu.au/ec/museums/col.html (accessed May 14, 2002), 2.
17. Suzi Gablik, *The Reenchantment of Art* (London: Thames and Hudson, 1992).
18. Suzi Gablik, *The Reenchantment of Art* (London: Thames and Hudson, 1992).
19. Tony Ellwood, "A Note from Tony Ellwood," in *Contemporary Art for Contemporary Kids* (Sherman Contemporary Art Foundation and Queensland Art Gallery, 2010), 44.

20. Barbara Piscitelli and Katrina Weier, "Learning with, through and about Art: The Role of social Interactions," in *Perspectives on Object-Centred Learning in Museums*, ed. Scott G. Paris, unpublished final report *QUT-Industry Collaborative Research Project* (Brisbane: Queensland University of Technology, 2002).
21. Lynne Seear, "Flexible Citizenship: The Art of Alfredo and Isabel Aquilizan," *Art in Australia Vol. 47/2: The 6th Asia-Pacific Triennial Contemporary Art Focus Issue* Summer (2009), 309.
22. Lynne Seear, "Flexible citizenship: The Art of Alfredo and Isabel Aquilizan."*Art in Australia Vol. 47/2: The 6th Asia-Pacific Triennial Contemporary Art Focus Issue* Summer (2009), 309.
23. Lynne Seear, "Flexible citizenship: The Art of Alfredo and Isabel Aquilizan."*Art in Australia Vol. 47/2: The 6th Asia-Pacific Triennial Contemporary Art Focus Issue* Summer (2009), 309.
24. Bob Hart, "Kids' APT — A Collaboration: Sponsorship in Review," *Tim Fairfax Family Foundation* (Queensland Art Gallery, 2009), 9.
25. Christine Nicholls in *APT6 in Review* (Brisbane: Queensland Art Gallery, 2010), 10.
26. Andrew Clark, "Contemporary Art for Contemporary Kids: In the Now and for the Future," in *Contemporary Art for Contemporary Kids* (Sherman Contemporary Art Foundation and Queensland Art Gallery, 2010), 36.

About the Author

Melina Mallos is Program Officer, Education and Curriculum Programs, at the Queensland Art Gallery | Gallery of Modern Art. For the past ten years, she has developed museum experiences for children, families, teachers and schools and initiated the popular Toddler Tuesday program in 2003. Melina's research interests focus on children's engagement with art. She was awarded a Queensland–Smithsonian Fellowship in 2009, where she investigated children's learning at the Smithsonian Early Enrichment Center.

From Classroom to Gallery

Building Community and Preserving Heritage

Kate Barron

Abstract When the levees broke during Hurricane Katrina in 2005, eighty percent of New Orleans flooded, and the citizens who returned to the evacuated city had to rebuild their homes, cultural institutions, and school system. This article records how The Ogden Museum of Southern Art, University of New Orleans, was able to collaborate with a charter school network to establish an early childhood enrichment program to benefit underserved children. In doing so, it realized the potential of a museum's ability to establish a community and pass on an artistic heritage

Building Community and Preserving Heritage

A major tenet of The Ogden Museum of Southern Art, University of New Orleans, a small regional museum in New Orleans, is that art is rooted in place, and the diverse Southern artists of all genres displayed within its walls do seem to be shaped by an attachment to place as well as narrative. Even those who turn to abstraction have a story to tell. For instance, Kenneth Shaw, a pattern and decoration artist, explains the bits of glass in *Sunship*, his painted tribute to John Coltrane, by saying, "I'm from New Orleans. I love glitter." This article describes the collaboration between The Ogden and the Capital One — UNO Charter School Network, which occurred in the aftermath of Hurricane Katrina, as evacuees returned to the devastated city to rebuild homes, businesses, cultural institutions, and a school system.

Journal of Museum Education, Volume 37, Number 1, Spring 2012, pp. 81–90.

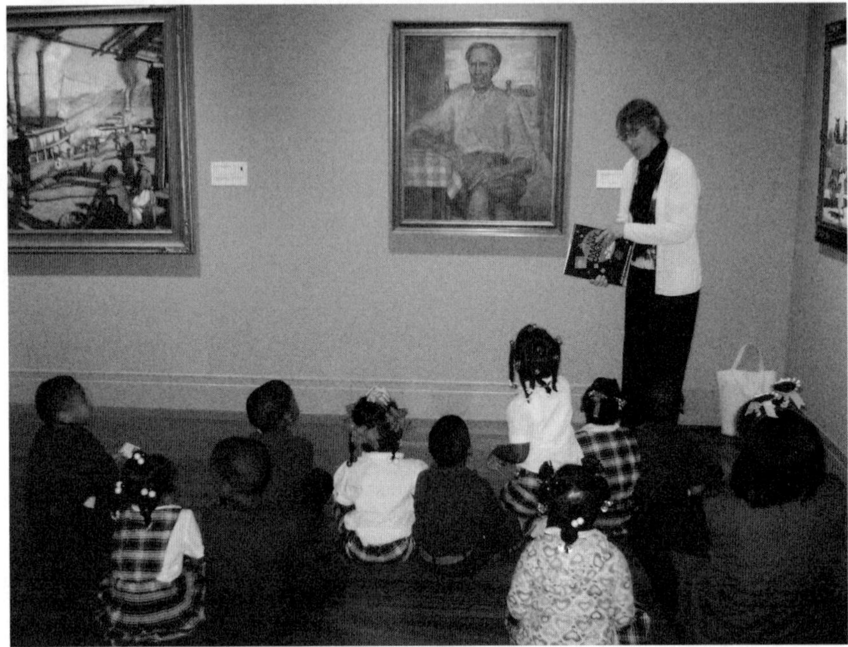

Discussion in the Gallery Pre-K students discuss the muted colors of Marie Atkinson Hull's *Tenant Farmer* (1935) before making an abstraction with boldly colored geometric paper shapes.

The fruit of that coming together of museum and school network is From Classroom to Gallery, an early childhood enrichment program. Following the Smithsonian Early Enrichment Center model, teachers of pre-kindergarten, kindergarten, and first grade in the three network schools use objects and prints that children can touch, describe, and explore to preview and review the oral reading of selected books. After the enhanced discussion of the books, the children visit The Ogden where in the galleries they encounter the art they saw in the prints and then engage in thematically related activities. Back at school they create art of their own. Each semester contains a From Classroom to Gallery unit, and at the end of the school year administrators, teachers, parents, and children attend an evening opening at the museum of the exhibition of the work they have created. In its fourth year, the program continues to enrich the lives of students no longer directly affected by the storm but whose world is fraught with blight and crime. Although how this warmly embraced program came into being is driven by the particulars of local experience, its basic structure can be used by other museum professionals.

The Collaborators: Museum and Schools

Ogden Museum of Southern Art, University of New Orleans is not an old institution. Conceived in 1994 as a public-private partnership with the University of New Orleans (UNO) to house the collection of Roger Ogden, it opened officially in August 2003. Director, J. Richard Gruber, and chief curator, David Houston, carried out the museum's mission to educate through exhibitions and programs about the art and culture of the South by celebrating its often overlooked diversity. Even before they moved into the museum's current building, they had hired education curators Anne Rowson Love and Debbie Randolph, who designed the enduring Artists and Sense of Place program, an artist residency for local elementary school children in grades two through five. Thus, after Katrina hit and the levees broke in August 2005, flooding 80% of the city and displacing its population, Gruber and Houston were predisposed to do what they could to help re-establish life in the city. On high ground, undamaged by the winds or water, The Ogden was the one of the first cultural institutions to reopen in the city in October 2005 with Ogden After Hours, its weekly music program on Thursday evenings.[1] That first night back more than six hundred people came to hear trumpeter James Andrews. They also got to hear his fiancée who spontaneously came out of the audience to join him in song, saying, "You really don't know what it means to miss New Orleans until you miss New Orleans."[2] In those first post-storm months Ogden After Hours programs continued to be reunions as more and more people were able to return home. The museum hosted several community planning sessions and exhibited architectural schemes, photographs documenting the destruction of the city, and the works of local artists responding to the experience. It was not until January 2007 that the museum felt it could move past Katrina-related exhibitions.[3]

In post-Katrina New Orleans, cultural institutions must navigate a complex system of school administration. The Orleans Parish School Board controls the schools that functioned well before the storm and survived relatively well after it; the rest are governed by the Recovery School District (RSD), a state entity created in 2003, the year of The Ogden's grand opening, and charged with taking over failing schools in the state. Failing school are those which for four years have a performance score of 60 or below, usually meaning 80% of students scored below Basic on the yearly LEAP (Louisiana Educational Assessment Program) test. The RSD's main strategy is to find groups willing to convert traditional failing schools to charter schools.[4] One such group was spearheaded by James Meza, Jr., Dean of the College of Education and Human Development at the University of New

Orleans, who believed the university should, "assume responsibility for the quality of public education in the New Orleans area." UNO's Charter School initiative became, in August 2004, the first organization in the state to take over a failing public school, Pierre A. Capdau. In August 2005, three days before Katrina hit, UNO opened its second charter, Medard H. Nelson.

Most of the city's schools were either physically damaged, some beyond repair, or depopulated by the evacuation. The RSD had to start building a school system practically from scratch. Both the UNO campus and Nelson were damaged by the storm, but the university managed to reopen the two charter schools in January and February 2006 with Nelson in temporary headquarters. In May 2006, Capital One Financial Corporation pledged $1 million to help establish the UNO Charter School Network, which by the fall of 2007, included a high school and another elementary school, Gentilly Terrace.[5] Capdeau, Nelson, and Gentilly Terrace are the three Network schools involved in the collaboration.

The Catalyst

Like Blanche DuBois in Tennessee Williams' *A Streetcar Named Desire*, New Orleans in her time of trouble depended on the kindness of strangers. A generous nation sent money and volunteers. Sharon Shaffer, Director of the Smithsonian Early Childhood Enrichment Center (SEEC), in town for the NAEA Convention in March 2008, sought out the local Smithsonian affiliate, The Ogden, to present a method of introducing young children to art in classrooms and museums. At the museum she found a staff of thirteen, down from twenty-seven before the storm, with a former high school English teacher filling in on a part-time, interim basis for the two education curators who had had to relocate after the storm. Since 2006, when the interim education coordinator joined the staff, she had been trying through collaboration with other cultural institutions and the museum's own programs to promote integration of the arts into the curriculum as a means of improving the education and spirits of all the city's children. The museum participated in teacher training, hosted teacher nights, ran its Artists and Sense of Place programs, and sponsored a high school writing contest for plays based on works in the collection. However, frustrations abounded. Teacher and principal turnover exacerbated by a fluctuating population (one school had four principals in three years) made it difficult to sustain any program. Teachers and administrators were reluctant to give over class time to the arts when they had to meet curricular benchmarks and prepare for the LEAP test. Many neighborhood schools had been destroyed by the storm, so children were bused to schools in parts of the city often far from their homes, and school budgets had little money left for field trip transportation. In addition, the consequences of the evacuation included months of missed schooling; some children missed as many as two full years of schooling. The enormity of the task of filling in the gaps the dislocation and fractured school system had caused was daunting to docents who found themselves spending precious time explaining basic facts and supplying vocabulary. Museum visits ceased to be engaging.

The SEEC art/museum/object-based curriculum seemed to be the ideal antidote to these frustrations. Working with the youngest students offered a fresh start, a way to build foundations in literacy so that children would not need remediation later. Since the LEAP test was in the relatively distant future for Pre-K and kindergarten children, teachers would be more open to field trips. And, because the SEEC model was well established, local administrators and teachers were more likely to embrace it. However, given the decentralized school system, finding a willing school would be difficult. Fortunately, through its UNO affiliation, the museum had the support of Vera Triplett, the brand new chief operating officer of the Capital One-UNO Charter School Network. In May 2008, the collaboration began with the decision to launch a pilot program. Dr. Shaffer returned to New Orleans in the fall of 2008 to present the SEEC philosophy to the administrators of the Network and the UNO Department of Education and Human Resources. She visited the schools to give demonstration lessons, led teacher and docent workshops at the museum, and designed two units. In January 2009, a month after full streetcar service was restored to the St. Charles Avenue line, the Pre-K and kindergarten children of the three collaborating schools came to the museum. The pilot program had begun following as closely as possible the Smithsonian model using The Ogden's collection.

Evolution

In the first year, both Pre-K and kindergarten shared the same curriculum. *Matthew's Dream*, the story of a mouse who discovers on a class visit to a museum that he wants to be an artist and then becomes one, was used to introduce the concept of a museum to the children. When they came to the museum, they were divided into small groups according to different colors and saw two paintings featuring whichever color was assigned to their group; red, blue, green, or yellow. They pretended to paint on canvas in the galleries and using Hunt Slonem's *Terrace Witness* as a model the students created art of their own by covering their drawings with patches of tissue paper. *Peter's Chair*, the story of a boy whose new baby sister is taking over all his old furniture, was used to extend the children's understanding of the possibilities of the meaning of "chair." The museum supplied two prints of chairs in the collection, one painted in patterns by self-taught artist George (Dot Man) Andrews, to enhance the discussion of the book in class. When the students came to the museum, they saw the originals of the two prints they had encountered in class, two other works featuring seated characters, and the exhibition of furniture by Randy Shull. In the galleries, they felt lace, denim, and driftwood, and listened to the music of Preservation Hall and Elvis Presley. The students then drew a piece of furniture and embellished it with a collage of scraps of paper and cloth. Another component of the program was creating museum play stations in the classrooms so that the children could pretend to be curators creating displays of objects or pictures. Although the children may not have recognized the salon style in which their works were hung in the first exhibition, visitors had the pleasure of studying an individual work or the delight of taking in a whole patterned wall. The treat of seeing the children view their work with their parents is one of the highlights of the year.

The Third Annual Exhibition took place in May 2011. Attendance had grown from about thirty parents and teachers the first year to over eighty, and the quality of the children's art had advanced to new levels. Dr. Triplett had au-

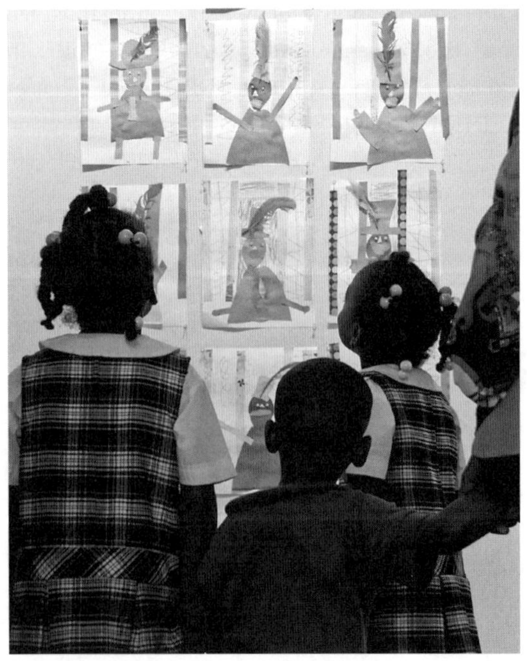

At the Opening At the 2010 exhibition, students and family members admire the Kindergarten's self-portraits with favorite hat.

thorized Jamie Jones, the art teacher at Nelson, and Renee Pierre, the art teacher at the Network's high school, to work with all three schools despite the logistical difficulties of meeting the Capdau Kindergarten and first grade in a New Orleans East church because their original building had been deemed unsafe and no other school site was available until Fall 2011 (such is the still shifting nature of school facilities in the city).

The resulting art projects were perfectly in keeping with the books for the spring. *Art From Her Heart* by Kathy Whitehead tells the story of Clementine Hunter, a Louisiana self-taught artist whose first painting was on a window shade as is her *Panorama of a Baptism* in The Ogden collection. Friends donated old advertising banners to Jones on the backs of which the first grade children painted scenes from their lives. In *The Room of Wonders* by Sergio Ruzzier, Pius Pelosi, the pack rat, collects found objects that he displays in his own gallery. The two art teachers made wooden "cabinets of wonders" that the children painted and filled with found objects. As Dr. Seuss's *My Many Colored Days* shows color expressing emotion, the Pre-K children made spirit houses by painting milk cartons they had brought to the art room from the cafeteria after lunch. This children's color exploration activity may seem relatively ordinary, but for Nelson students it assumes special meaning. The school is situated just off DeSaix Circle where a sculpture, *Spirit House*, by John Scott stands. Incorporating drawings by earlier Nelson students, this 2002 piece honors the contributions of unnamed African Americans to the building and culture of New Orleans. In the Pre-K

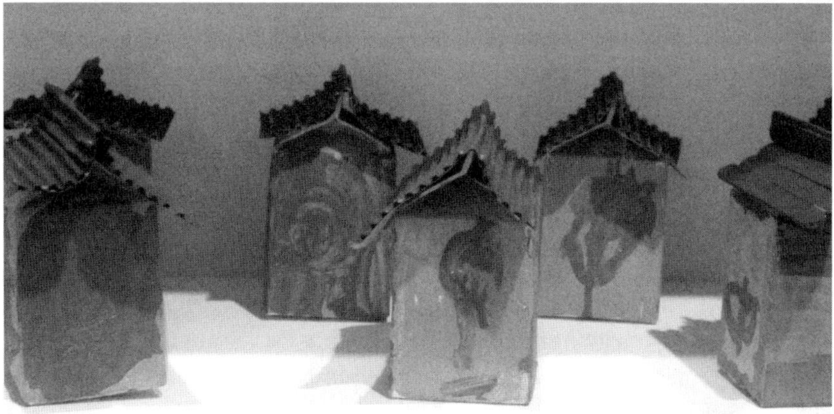

Spirit Houses Pre-K students chose three colors to represent their feelings and painted a house to honor their ancestors. Even in black and white the artworks' natural exuberance and the students' delight in the project are apparent.

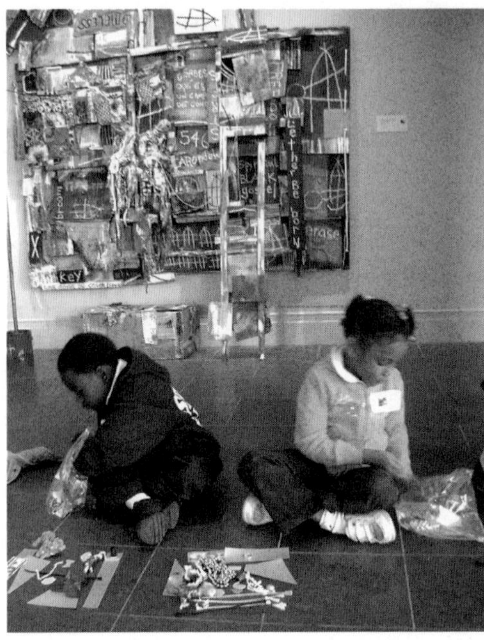

Creating in the Gallery Inspired by *Makin' of a Melody* by Jeffrey Cook (1961–2009), first graders at the museum make collages with found objects.

project, Jones honors Scott, the man who was his teacher at Xavier University, the revered artist who died in Houston in September 2007 after evacuating because of Katrina.

Benefits

Of particular importance that first year was the nature of the museum experience for both teachers and students. The majority of art on display at the Ogden is twentieth or twenty-first century with several living artists represented. The work is colorful and often textured; the artists formally trained or self taught. The building is intimate with three floors of galleries in which numerous works by African American artists or with African American subjects appear. The children are able not only to see their own world represented, but also hear stories about living artists from docents who have met them. The children can engage in a music listening activity in front of a portrait of a Preservation Hall musician. They can connect to a landscape not only because it depicts a familiar levee but also because it was painted by the architect of the museum, who happens to be the husband of "Miss Kate," the education coordinator. When first grade was added to the program, the children read Faith Ringgold's *Tar Beach*, whose narrator views the George Washington Bridge from her New York City tenement rooftop. Their "brick beach" was The Ogden's rooftop terrace with a view of the bridge over the Mississippi River.

Museum etiquette helped teachers maintain discipline in the classroom as the museum visits demanded order. "Use your museum voice" became a standard instruction in the schools.

The museum provided serenity. During the in-gallery activities the children were silent as they arranged bits of denim and lace on a page. In the quiet of The Andrews-Humphrey Family Gallery, they imitated a painted plower and waved to each other over the planted field they had made with crepe paper streamers and artificial leaves. They wanted to come to the museum, a special place where they belonged. The museum workshops gave faculty an enriching respite, built camaraderie, and helped unify the curriculum of the three schools. The museum became something of a sanctuary in a crime-ridden city. As Dr. Triplett said to the parents gathered at the 2011 exhibition opening, "Consider what happens on the streets and look where your children are now."

Logistics

The Network provided necessary administrative support in the form of transportation, substitutes for teachers during training sessions, and, most importantly, a liaison. Having one person with authority to coordinate the three schools turned out to be crucial, but Karen Gauthier, the literacy coach, went beyond logistics. She filled in as a museum docent for the field trips, performed demonstration lessons in the schools, and, with The Ogden's education coordinator, presented a workshop in the third year for teachers new to the program.

Learning the SEEC techniques of using objects and art to expand a child's understanding of words was transformative for the New Orleanians involved. As one teacher said on the first year's evaluation form, using objects and art prints to stimulate discussion and observation, "was practical and could be part of our teaching day." Docents loved the technique of in-gallery activities to supplement the comparison of books and works of art and were impressed by the improved level of discourse from the first to the second Pre-K museum visits. Success could also be seen in the readiness with which Gentilly Terrace second graders this year recalled details from *Tar Beach* the year before and spoke excitedly about making the bridge with their bodies on the brick beach of the rooftop terrace.

Outside expertise lent authority to the program but more importantly it helped bring school and museum staffs together as workshop participants, a common experience that formed the basis for warm and cordial relationships.

Initial training sessions and yearly planning get-togethers have made teachers an important part of the program and keep museum staff alert to the actual problems and curricular needs of the schools, grounding them in the children's world.

Conclusion

This recounting of how a small museum, in the aftermath of an enormous storm was able "to respond to the aspirations and needs of citizens in their communities"[6] is written in tribute to the administrators, principals, teachers, and museum docents who worked together with such good results. What happened in New Orleans almost by chance, however, can happen by design in other cities contending with social and economic blight. A program like From Classroom to Gallery can provide a model for successful teaching methods. It can give children who are not exposed to books or art at home another world. It can connect a local audience to local artistic traditions. It can assure children that their own lives are worthy of art. Approximately three hundred children, of whom ninety per cent receive free or reduced price lunch, participated in the first three years of the program. They had never been to a museum before the program began, but they are members now of a museum/school family and recognize themselves as Southern artists.

Notes

1. Esker, Frtiz. "Warehouse District Museums Overcome Damage, Looting from Katrina." *New Orleans CityBusiness*. Jan 30, 2006. http://findarticles.com/p/articles/mi_qn4200/is_20060130/ai_n16031240/
2. Ogden Museum of Southern Art archives.
3. See The Ogden website for a listing of post-Katrina exhibitions and programs www.ogdenmuseum.org.
4. Louisiana Recovery School District, http://www.rsdla.net/Home.aspx.
5. In July 2011 the Capital One UNO Charter School Network became the Capital One New Beginnings Network. The facts of the history of the network outlined in this article remain on the new website: http://www.newbeginningsnola.net/apps/pages/index.jsp?uREC_ID=123088&type=d&pREC_ID=257005
6. AAM Board of Directors. "AAM Museums and Community Resolution." http://www.aam-us.org/sp/m-and-c-board-resol.cfm?renderforprint=1

About the Author

Having just retired from twenty-nine years of teaching English and Humanities at Isidore Newman School in New Orleans, Kate Barron joined the staff of The Ogden Museum of Southern Art in September 2006. A 1967 graduate of Vassar College with an M.A.T from Tulane University, she rebuilt The Ogden's education department in the wake of Hurricane Katrina.

Museums and Community

The Benefits of Working Together

K. Allison Wickens

Abstract This case study of "Listen, Look, & Do," a multi-visit preschool program at the Smithsonian's National Postal Museum, provides a model for how other history museums can program for young learners in their neighborhoods. In striving to meet local community audience needs identified by annual evaluations, staff created a program that shifted its focus from prioritizing the museum's content to improving the learners' experience. While still rooted in postal themes and objects, the program's key benefits to teachers and students emerge from the skill- and place-based modifications we made. This signature program's structure now informs all offerings developed by the National Postal Museum education department, as it seeks first to be for someone, and second to be about something.

In early childhood, when kids are finding new opportunities to express and understand themselves, repeat visits to a local museum can provide a familiar environment to explore and make sense of the world.[1] At the National Postal Museum, we offer the program "Listen, Look, & Do" to meet this need. In an era defined by audience-centered missions and initiatives, transforming a program to meet the needs of the visitor has become a core part of many museums' operations.[2] Our steps taken to give kids a program that supports their emotional and social comfort have allowed us to broaden the mission of our educational offerings and to frame the museum's historic content in new ways. Educators at the National Postal Museum, like our colleagues at other museums, are keenly aware of trends in museum practice. These modes of thinking inform our programming choices and priorities and lead to programs that embrace the call to be for someone, not

Journal of Museum Education, Volume 37, Number 1, Spring 2012, pp. 91–100.

about something.[3] Attention to local teacher and student needs transformed the education mission from teaching discipline-based content to creating a space that promotes learning in accessible and meaningful ways. This new programming model includes great content, but is not dependent upon it.

Once relegated to traditional school tours, or even discouraged from visiting, the needs and interests of kids now inform many museum projects and exhibits; dedicated exhibit spaces, specialized programming, and targeted marketing to children under eight flourish. Initially deemed as radical or unnecessary, discovery centers and hands-on rooms now serve an essential role for any museum hoping to serve family or school audiences.[4] Birthday and slumber party programs remain important revenue generators and bring in young visitors, tying the museum-going experience with positive life-defining moments.[5] Blockbuster exhibitions sell family-friendly items in museum shops to broaden their appeal.[6] Even within the school tour format, new audience-centered considerations must meet teacher requirements to be standards-based, multi-modal, and engaging.[7]

At the National Postal Museum, our understanding of young children's needs increased from the multiple visit approach. Our decision to target local schools — which can access the museum more frequently and cheaply — built the foundation for meaningful community involvement. Recent scholarship has illustrated the ways in which neighborhood-based programming can impact all parties involved. Whether redefining their spaces as social forums, exhibiting their collections through community voices, or developing programs with an eye for visitor investment, museums have reaped tangible and intangible rewards through community involvement.[8]

With classes returning month after month and year after year, the "Listen, Look, & Do" programs use diverse interpretation techniques to create strong relationships between students, objects, exhibits, staff, and teachers. The summative evaluation conducted by an external evaluator, shows that the multiple trip model not only provides preschool students with opportunities to create personal connections to the museum, but also reinforces classroom learning, fosters new skills, and encourages fun.[9] Other research supports that multiple visit programs like these can build comfort and increase learning for community members at the museum.[10] This program's success generated the confidence for the Postal Museum to adopt a project-development process that more readily incorporates audience needs into new and revised education programs and materials. In embracing this mission-level change, we have strengthened the museums' offerings for more than just the community's youngest visitors. Still, our programming for them remains our touchstone for success.

Key Features of "Listen, Look, & Do" ...A Program's Beginning

This museum has always been characterized as "kid-friendly," but programs did not differentiate between children on vacation and those that lived locally. Staff members perceived visitors as mainly out of town tourists, stamp collectors, and postal employees, which influenced the museum's programming agenda. That didn't keep the nearby neighbors from coming. Immediately surrounding the museum is an urban neighborhood. Capitol Hill is the location of our nation's legislative and judicial branches of government, but encircling these iconic buildings is a rich and diverse residential community. First-time homebuyers and public housing residents raise and educate their young children in the mile surrounding the Postal Museum. Federal buildings and downtown campuses even house preschools for their commuting employees and students.

Within the early years of the museum's life, savvy educators in area schools and day care centers recognized that the Postal Museum was an inviting place for their classes to explore. Free admission, ease of access, relatively low visitor flow, and large, kid-friendly objects all contributed to the Postal Museum's selection as a repeat destination. After attending the only tour for preschools, "Let's Deliver Mail!," local groups continued to return despite the lack of facilitated options. These groups came to the Postal Museum for more than the opportunity to dress like postal workers and pretend to deliver letters. In 2005, after informal interviews with returning teachers, we created a multi-visit program featuring varied interpretation of our key themes and signature objects that four-year-olds cherish.

Famous bandleader Duke Ellington is a DC-hometown favorite and the subject of February's Black History Month "Listen, Look, & Do" program. After participating in an interactive telling of the book *Duke Ellington: The Piano Prince & His Orchestra*, students explore the themes of transportation, music, teamwork, and diversity as they visit objects in the gallery including a Duke Ellington postage stamp and a full-sized train car.[11] Students have the opportunity to improve skills and knowledge in reading, math, and music by using image, sound, and their bodies to compare and contrast musical instruments and tempos mentioned in the story. In the culminating activity children get instruments and all create music together. The theme of diversity in the broadest sense (different instruments make different sounds) ties this program to Black History Month topics in ways that young people can grasp.[12]

This brief illustration of one program's structure highlights the key features that tie the "Listen, Look, & Do" series together. Over the years, the program has changed to address visitor needs, but the following core qualities have remained constant: Students *listen* to a story, *look* at objects, and *do* an activity. Multiple intelligence theory informs the interpretive strategies used within the familiar three-mode structure (story/tour/activity). Within this traditional programming model, we use the story to build diverse connections from the plot and characters to the authentic objects and experiences in the museum.

The Program and the Museum Transform

During the first year, we focused our efforts on achieving two museum priorities: to teach kids about the Postal Museum and create an environment that is comfortable and fun for them. We continue to balance these dual goals to provide students with a foundation for learning history and visiting museums. However, we have revised the program in three waves in response to participant evaluations and surveys (both internal and externally administered). The first modification altered the content. Initially we saw "Listen, Look, & Do" as an opportunity to teach participants more about our museum themes. But four and five-year-olds struggled to grasp the historical concepts that contextualize the objects that we explore with older students and adults. With this hurdle identified, we realized that young children's love for the museum and history was not tied to content acquisition, and could be gained by ensuring that they were engaged in meaningful and enjoyable experiences. Expressing themselves with confidence proved to be more immediately effective in creating a fun environment than pacing them through the steps a letter takes to go through the mail.

In the second wave of revisions, participating school teachers helped us identify and give primacy to preschool-age skill-development elements existing in repeated programs. Focusing on colors, patterns, emotions, and story structure created more continuity between the monthly themes, and ultimately more potential for building upon students' existing knowledge and classroom experiences. Our third-wave revisions have allowed the museum to capitalize on the school groups' locale by highlighting place-based lessons that illuminate our Capitol Hill neighborhood as a learning space. This is reinforced by repeat journeys between the museum and the school.

Each wave has brought both concrete programmatic change and incremental philosophical shifts in the pull between audience needs and museum content. As the program has changed to better serve local audience needs, Postal Museum content has not been set adrift. Students now engage with content in age-appropriate ways and make their own meaning out of broader themes. A train car is no longer defined as a big metal box that carried the mail, but as a jazz-swinging metal box that inspired a musician to cross boundaries. While interpretations meet at the core historical idea that trains travel and link people, places, and information, the latter better achieves the museum's objective to engage young learners and build key life skills.

Benefits to the Students

The students who attend our programs come from diverse economic and cultural backgrounds, which do not always fit into traditional museum-going categories. Staff of cultural institutions care about people becoming life-long museum goers; studies show that children who attend museums are more likely to become adult visitors.[13] We hypothesize that this program will have a long-term effect on the participants but have not yet conducted any longitudinal studies.

In a formal yearlong study conducted in 2007–08, we saw notable changes in how kids from a local public school defined the museum in relation to themselves and their peers.[14] In the beginning of the school year (before their first tour) 71% of the case study group (n=10) did not draw anything related to a museum when asked what they thought about when they heard the word "museum." Only 21% could give a fair or moderately detailed verbal description of a museum. One child, when asked to explain his artwork, said, "mine's a monster!"

By the end of the school year, after approximately seven visits, students were better able to express their familiarity with museums, and, not surprisingly, focused almost exclusively on the National Postal Museum in both their words and pictures.[15] In the artistic evidence, children included themselves and their friends engaging with objects, activities, and exhibitions specific to their Postal Museum experiences. Students demonstrated much more familiarity with the museum post-test, and were able to draw and describe details of objects, exhibits, activities, and the museum building itself. Data from teacher interviews also suggested that the consistent routine of reading a story, then moving into the gallery, and then returning for a creative activity, helped children feel a sense of comfort and familiarity with the program because they could "predict" the experience, and thus have some sense of control. Other elements that seemed to support children's comfort level was the use of familiar activities (story time and art-making), and the presence of the same staff member for each visit.[16] Together, data from students and teachers suggest that we improved not only their knowledge of museums, but also their comfort within them, or at least specifically within the National Postal Museum. Memories of museums benefit from increased time in the museum, familiar presentation methods, and a positive social environment.[17]

Comfort in a learning environment is strongly linked to the ability to build new knowledge on pre-existing experiences.[18] As we worked to revise our program based on its first formal evaluation, we recognized that some of our content goals had no grounding in the children's daily lives. March's Women's History Month program features a story about airmail pilot Amelia Earhart.[19] In the first few years we wanted the students to understand that women flew planes and that those planes carried mail, but these knowledge-based outcomes were outside of the young students' experiences. We saw a dramatic increase in student participation when we changed the interpretation of the story to be about the pilot's emotions and feelings while in flight. By reframing the learning goals to support more age-appropriate skills like analyzing textures and expressing emotions, we simultaneously increased student engagement and helped teachers develop their students' critical thinking skills.

Over the years, we have discovered that teachers and students started the visit long before their classes physically arrived at the museum. Rarely do schools organize unprompted pre-visit activities, but because the Postal Museum was a repeat destination, some teachers made their actual journey a lesson in itself to support the museum program. Altered by weather and seasons, each trip contained new experiences overlaying a familiar walk. Tying place-based education to the museum's program enriches the students' learning experience and helps them solidify the museum as a neighborhood destination.[20] To capitalize on this opportunity, we changed our interpretation of the November book: *Arrow to the Sun*.[21] The activities and tour now compare and contrast the Capitol Hill neighborhood with the American Southwest environment by placing adjacent dramatic canyon illustrations and neighborhood federal buildings. This links the scenery of the story's journey to the architecture seen during the students' walk — helping them contextualize the concept of environment. By integrating both skill-based outcomes and place-based education features into a program designed to generate comfort in young visitors, the museum provides learners with rich repeat visits that build sustaining museum memories.

Benefits to Teachers

We survey teachers annually. The results have confirmed our conclusions that the program benefits students. Teachers also assess the value of programs such as "Listen, Look, & Do" by their ability to help them achieve classroom goals.

Teachers have identified our use of multiple techniques to convey the themes as particularly meaningful.[22] Using different modes of learning, these programs inspire active, vocal, social, introspective, and creative expressions from the student participants. After multiple visits, these methods can even be tailored as the designated museum educator gains knowledge of individual students' preferences for and struggles over certain tasks and skills.

A 2007 grant allowed us to give each participating class a copy of a featured book. Teachers used this tool to extend the museum experience to lessons in the classroom. In every instance but one, all teachers who participated in the subsequent external evaluation study reported that they re-read the stories in the classroom.[23] Teachers reinforced the program in additional ways, including discussions, activities, and games related to the monthly theme. One teacher reported that she even sent the books home with students on a rotating basis so that the kids could share tales of the trips with their families.

Before the 2011–12 school year, we conducted a marketing survey and subsequently began offering each program year-round. Previously, we had aligned each program with a month, using federally designated heritage months as a guideline. However, local teachers use different criteria to organize their school year. Often, they didn't teach a unit that linked to the tour during the month that we offered it. Misaligned themes meant that teachers would not be able to attend programs best suited to their classrooms purely because of timing. We now offer a slate of six programs available across the eight months of the school year. Teachers can pick the theme of their choice when it best suits their curriculum.

Participants Transform Museum Practice

Open communication between the museum and teacher partners ensures a strong reputation for quality school programming in our neighborhood. Each year we hire a part-time educator to build strong ties with the students and teachers as she or he schedules, facilitates, and reflects on each visit. This staff member gains expertise in community needs that can be applied to other museum projects beyond preschool tours. The museum has developed a stronger interpretive toolbox for many of the signature objects on the tours because we can see how children's interactions with them change month to month. Awareness of the opinions, reactions, and preferences of these pint-sized visitors influences public programming and exhibition development decisions. For example, direct experiences with community youth and educators have shaped both our plans for the museum's new welcome center, as well as the start times of our family-oriented programs.[24]

The most unexpected impact of "Listen, Look, & Do" has been on our conceptual model for school tours and curriculum materials. Five years ago, the education department staff would not conduct programs or create curriculum that did not have historic or philatelic-themed content as a primary focus. Today, inspired by "Listen, Look, & Do," our new materials use postal-based themes as thought-provoking interpretive lenses for developing a myriad of 21st-century skills. This approach gives our education products, teacher trainings, and programming new life and relevance in today's and tomorrow's classrooms. For example, while Amelia Earhart's historical and philatelic significance are inherently interesting and important to many visitors, her story truly gains relevance to children when they meet her in a lesson that directly relates to their daily experiences with emotions and the five senses.

Another transformative benefit of "Listen, Look, & Do" is the doors it has opened between the museum and the Capitol Hill community. As part of the Smithsonian Institution, we have a mandate to serve all the residents of the United States, but our commitment to nearby young visitors increases our involvement with and understanding of the adults and children who live in the surrounding neighborhood. While most of our visitation will continue to be tourists from outside of Washington, DC, our service to them is now balanced with marketing and programming efforts that benefit locals.

Conclusions

Our concern with young learners and the subsequent development of "Listen, Look, & Do" helped launch a museum initiative to better serve the residents of Capitol Hill. Born out of teacher-initiatives, our evaluations and surveys have shown that the program has offered notable benefits for participants each year. Our commitment to collecting and implementing feedback based on thoughtful and meaningful data has built a program that is mutually beneficial. The neighborhood proximity of the participants and the repeat nature of the program contribute to the vested interest both the museum and the visitors have in the program's success and lessons learned.

Exhibits at the Postal Museum tell historic stories. Young children are just beginning to comprehend the meaning of history as something that previously happened, but they lack many of the skills required to put these stories in a chronological timeframe. Often, museums shy away from giving kids history experiences because their capacity for understanding the past is different from adults. But the success of this program illustrates one way that history museums can provide a rich learning environment for young children. Our institution has created positive museum and history-related moments by focusing on student needs instead of museum objects.

"Listen, Look & Do" offers an example of how museums can act as agents of change in the world of education.[25] By helping connect historical objects to children's own experiences, repeat programs like this can provide fertile ground for students' future lessons. Working directly with schools in close regional proximity increases the opportunity to make a profound impact on the local community. In turn, this regularity informs our museum practice by giving us a group of repeat visitors to evaluate. To achieve improvement, education programmers must value the needs of the audience and modify or refine their guiding missions from a content focus to one that is process-based. If museum practitioners *listen* to learners within their own community and *look* for ways their programs can serve them best, educators can *do* great things for their own institutions and the young learners who grow comfortable in museum spaces.

Notes

1. George E. Hein and Mary Alexander, *Museums: Places of Learning* (Washington, DC: American Associations of Museums, 1998), 11.
2. Stephen E. Weil, *Making Museums Matter* (Washington, DC: Smithsonian Institution Press, 2002), 49.
3. Ibid., 28.
4. Sally Osberg, "Shared Lessons and Self Discoveries: What Research has Taught Children's Discovery Museums," *Journal of Museum Education* 23, no. 1 (1998): 19.
5. Betsy Bowers and Rebecca Fulcher, "Seeing Potential, Pushing Possibilities: Thinking Creatively about Revenue Opportunities," *Journal of Museum Education* 35, no. 2 (2010): 178.
6. Julia Beizer, Susan Breitkopf, and Amanda Litvinov, "Marketing the King: Tut 2 and the New Blockbuster," *Museum News* November/December (2005): 41.
7. Mary Ellen Flannery, "'It Can't Just be Fun' What Teachers want from Field Trips," Museum March/April (2009): 47.
8. Elaine Heumann Gurian, "Offering Safer Public Spaces," *Journal of Museum Education* 20, no. 3 (1995): 14; Deborah Schwartz, "Experiments in Making History Personal: Public Discourse, Complexity, and Community Building," *Journal of Museum Education* 35, no. 1 (2010): 73–74; Betsy Bowers and Rebecca Fulcher, "Seeing Potential, Pushing Possibilities: Thinking Creatively about Revenue Opportunities," *Journal of Museum Education* 35, no. 2 (2010): 179.
9. Jill Stein and Claudia Figueiredo 'Listen, Look & Do' Program Evaluation Report. Technical evaluation report. Edgewater, MD: Institute for Learning Innovation. (2008). www.npm.si.edu/industrywhitepapers/Listen_Look_and_Do_Evaluation_Report.pdf.
10. George E. Hein, *Learning in the Museum* (New York, NY: Routledge, 2001), 34.
11. Andrea Pinkney and Brian Pinkney, *Duke Ellington: The Piano Prince & His Orchestra* (New York, NY: Hyperion Books-Children, 2006).
12. Jill Stein and Claudia Figueiredo *'Listen, Look & Do' Program Evaluation Report*. (2008). www.npm.si.edu/industrywhitepapers/Listen_Look_and_Do_Evaluation_Report.pdf.

13. Betty Farrell and Maria Medvedeva, *Demographic Transformation and the Future of Museums* (Washington, DC: American Associations of Museums, 2010), 14.
14. Jill Stein and Claudia Figueiredo *'Listen, Look & Do' Program Evaluation Report.* (2008). www.npm.si.edu/industrywhitepapers/Listen_Look_and_Do_Evaluation_Report.pdf.
15. Not all children attended all seven visits due to absences, illness, etc.; Jill Stein and Claudia Figueiredo *'Listen, Look & Do' Program Evaluation Report.* (2008). www.npm.si.edu/industrywhitepapers/Listen_Look_and_Do_Evaluation_Report.pdf.
16. Ibid., www.npm.si.edu/industrywhitepapers/Listen_Look_and_Do_Evaluation_Report.pdf.
17. John H. Falk and Lynn D. Dierking, "Recalling the Museum Experience," *Journal of Museum Education* 20, no. 2 (1995):13.
18. George Hein, *Learning in the Museum*, 34.
19. Pam Munoz Ryan, *Amelia and Eleanor Go For a Ride* (New York, NY: Scholastic, 1999).
20. David A. Gruenewald, Nancy Koppelman, and Anna Elam, "Our place in History," *Journal of Museum Education* 32 (2007): 234.
21. Gerald McDermott, *Arrow to the Sun* (New York, NY: Penguin Publishing Group, 1977).
22. Jill Stein and Claudia Figueiredo *'Listen, Look & Do' Program Evaluation Report.* (2008). www.npm.si.edu/industrywhitepapers/Listen_Look_and_Do_Evaluation_Report.pdf.
23. Ibid., www.npm.si.edu/industrywhitepapers/Listen_Look_and_Do_Evaluation_Report.pdf.
24. The Postal Museum's entry lobby has been called by the teachers as "imposing" especially considering how kid-friendly it is once you get to the exhibits. In renovation of the entrance scheduled for 2013, we are integrating graphics and lighting to make it more inviting to families and schools. We now start all our family festivals two hours earlier to hit the pre-lunch/pre-nap time.
25. Beverly Sheppard, "Insistent Questions in our Learning Age," *Journal of Museum Education* 35 (2010): 225.

About the Author

K. Allison Wickens leads the education department at the Smithsonian's National Postal Museum. Her professional expertise lies in informal education, interpretive technology, and practical evaluation. She received a master's degree in history and a certificate in museum studies from the University of Colorado, Boulder.

Uncovering Visitor Identity

A Citywide Utilization of the Falk Visitor-Identity Model

Laureen Trainer, Marley Steele-Inama, and Amber Christopher

Abstract In his book, *Identity and the Museum Visitor Experience*, John Falk makes the case that by understanding the underlying motivations that drive a visitor, a museum can create an experience that reflects a person's identity and therefore satisfy their motivation for visiting. According to Falk, this level of personal connection increases meaningfulness to the visit. This, in turn, helps a museum develop and sustain a community of learners, and ultimately attendance and revenue. A network of nine cultural institutions in Denver utilized Falk's instrument to gain a "snap-shot" of what motivates museum-goers in one metropolitan community. The study, which employed the Falk Visitor Identity-Related Motivation Typology, and its results, is presented in this article. Further, Denver Zoo outlines how it has used the data from the Falk study to rethink and enhance staff professional development, program development and learning outcomes, and marketing.

The Background

In 2009, John Falk released his much-anticipated *Identity and the Museum Visitor Experience*. With this book, Falk claims to have moved beyond demographic descriptions; female, Hispanic, age 32, for example, as the primary indicator of "knowing a visitor." Rather, he identifies and categorizes the motivational needs and roles engendered by underlying identities that can be used as a predictive model of visitor experience. He purports that this model can aid museum professionals in better meeting the needs of their visitors. In the model, he sets forth five identities that define a visitor's motivation for attending a cultural institution: ex-

Journal of Museum Education, Volume 37, Number 1, Spring 2012, pp. 101–114.

plorer, facilitator, professional/hobbyist, experience seeker, and recharger.[1] The premise is that by understanding the underlying motivations that drive a visitor, a museum can create an experience that reflects a person's identity and therefore satisfy his or her motivation for visiting. According to Falk, this level of personal connection increases meaningfulness. This, in turn, helps to develop and sustain a community of learners, and ultimately attendance and revenue.

In his book, Falk acknowledges and discusses some previous visitor motivation research and typologies, most of which have been based in leisure research. One of the earliest leisure researchers, John Kelly (1977), argued that people engaged in cultural activities based on what they believed they would recoup from the experience; for example, if a mother or father believe that good parents take their child(ren) to museums then they would visit museums with their child(ren) in order to feel like good parents.[2] In 1980, leisure researchers Jacob Beard and Mounir G. Ragheb posited six components of perceived motivation for leisure (psychology, educational, social, relaxation, physiological, and aesthetic).[3] In 1996, Michael James Manfredo and Beverly L. Driver described 15 major overarching motivations that drive leisure and recreational behaviors; however, Falk poses the question in *Identity and the Museum Visitor Experience*, "Many of these categories could easily apply to museum-going, but which ones?" A review of the literature indicates a small subset of researchers that specifically have looked at museum visitor motivation (Hood, 1981; Bigley, et al, 1992; Moussouri, 1997; Packer, & Ballantyne, 2002; Yalowitz, 2002).[4] The motivation typologies range broadly from Informational Reasoning and Sensory Reasoning for Visiting (Yalowitz, 2002) to distinct categories of visitor motivations, such as museum researchers Jan Packer and Roy Ballentyne's (2002) categories of: 1) learning and discovery; 2) passive enjoyment; 3) restoration; 4) social interaction; and 5) self-fulfillment. For the purpose of this study, the authors focused specifically on Falk's five categorical motivation identity typologies, as it represented the latest emergence of museum visitor motivation typology theories in the field.

Falk used this past research and the results of a multi-year, multi-layered research project at California Science Center initiated in 2000 that he conducted with Martin Storksdieck, to come up with a new understanding of motivations based on little "i" identities.[5] These identities differ from capital "I" identities, which are fixed, such as age and ethnic background/heritage, as two examples. Little "i" identities are fluid, and are often situational and contextual.[6] For instance, when a block-buster exhibition debuts at a local art museum, a patron might visit on Friday evening hoping to be excited/inspired/impressed. In this case the visitor is an explorer. However, when he visits the local zoo with his nieces and nephews the following day and ensures that his family has the best experience possible, he assumes the role of a facilitator. And finally, on Sunday, he takes a tour of an orchid exhibition at the botanic gardens, as he hopes to gain information on improving the health of his own orchids, he has transformed into a professional/hobbyist. In this case, one museum-goer adopted three identity motivations over the course of a weekend. Falk argues that unlike fixed, demographic identities, little "i" identities have a greater impact on day-to-day decision making, like the decision to visit a particular museum on a particular day. In addition, a visitor's expectations and needs vary according to his or her motivation to attend a museum. Was the visitor impressed by the blockbuster exhibition? Did his nieces and nephews have fun and learn? Did he learn something about orchids? Therefore satisfaction is a product of whether those specific and changing needs were met.

Using the results of his research to frame his theory, Falk introduced five identity-related motivational types in *Identity and the Museum Visitor Experience*.[7]

- **Explorers** are curiosity-driven with a generic interest in the content of the museum. They expect to find something that will grab their attention and fuel their learning.
- **Facilitators** are socially motivated. Their visit is focused on primarily enabling the experience and learning of others in their accompanying social group.
- **Professional/hobbyists** feel a close tie between the museum content and their professional or hobbyist passions. Their visits are typically motivated by a desire to satisfy a specific content related objective.
- **Experience Seekers** are motivated to visit because they perceive the museum as an important destination. Their satisfaction primarily derives from the mere fact of having "been there and done that."
- **Rechargers** are primarily seeking to have a contemplative, spiritual and/or restorative experience; they use the museum as a refuge from the work-a-day world.[8]

Some museum professionals have expressed admiration for Falk's ideas, such as Roy Ballantyne, University of Queensland, and editor of *Visitor Studies Today*. Ballantyne wrote: "This book should be read by anyone serious about visitor experiences in museums. Falk reconceptualises [sic] the field from a wholistic [sic] perspective using the 'lens' of visitor identity and motivation. The model he proposes will shape and inform the nature, design and understanding of visitor experiences in free-choice learning environments."[9] However, a larger segment of the museum and visitor studies field has spent more time focusing on the shortcomings of the book. Many, including Adam Bickford, a trained sociologist and former analyst for the Institutional Studies Office at the Smithsonian Institution, in his review for *Curator*, have pointed out that there are not enough data to support Falk's conclusions: "I have tried to understand the methods and findings supporting the authors' conclusions: who participated in the study, what kinds of questions were participants asked, how were the responses analyzed, how were categories defined, and how do those definitions contribute to the understanding of visitors and visits? . . . Unfortunately, my answer to the *How do[es] the [author] know this?* question has to be, 'I have no idea.'"[10]

Staff members of the Visitor Research and Program Evaluation Department at the Denver Museum of Nature & Science (DMNS) read *Identity and the Museum Visitor Experience* and agreed with many of the commentaries surrounding the murky methodology and somewhat unconventional definitions of identity; however, researchers also saw Falk's book as a call to action. DMNS located the instrument Falk used, got out on the floor at the DMNS, and surveyed its visitors. Researchers found that visitors could choose a card that reflected their dominant reason for visiting DMNS that day. From this successful finding, research staff came up with bigger ideas of using the Falk Visitor Identity-Related Motivation Typology instrument at other cultural institutions in Denver to develop a citywide perspective of what motivates people in the Denver Metropolitan Area (Denver Metro) area to visit museums. Working with a recently formed network of museum professionals involved in evaluation, DMNS partnered with several institutions throughout Denver to launch one, large study.

The Methodology

The research questions driving the study were: Which motivation type is dominant at each of the institutions, and did the motivation types differ among different cultural institutions? In addition, the citywide project also had the aim of creating evaluation capacity in institutions as well as developing a community of institutional learners in one city who would have a common vocabulary and data set from which to understand visitors. A final goal of the project was for each institution to take the data back to its museum and develop innovative and personalized ways of turning the data set into effective ways to engage with visitors and to keep refining the visitors' museum experience.

Over the course of two and a half months during the summer of 2010, the Falk instrument was employed at nine different cultural institutions: the Buffalo Bill Museum and Grave, Butterfly Pavilion, Children's Museum of Denver, Denver Art Museum, Denver Botanic Gardens, Denver Zoo, DMNS, Molly Brown House Museum, and Wildlife Experience. All a part of the Scientific and Cultural Facilities District (SCFD) in the Denver Metro area, these nine museums represent a wide array of size, budgets, and content.

The study ran on one weekday (either a Wednesday or Thursday) and one weekend day (either a Saturday or Sunday) at each institution in an effort to gather a wide sample of Denver Metro visitors. The Falk instrument consists of 20 cards that each contain a picture and a phrase (for the purpose of the study, researchers printed the cards on 8.5 x 5.5 inches cardstock and in color). The 20 cards are evenly divided into the five motivational categories. One card, as an example, presents an image of two adults in a greenhouse where one adult appears to be explaining something to the other, and includes the saying, "It relates to the kind of work I do and I find it useful" in a word bubble. This is an example of a professional/hobbyist motivation. One of the facilitator cards features the backs of a mother and father as they point out features of a modern sculpture to their two daughters. This card includes, "My family/friends learn things here they can't in other places," and is an example of a facilitator motivation.[11]

A team of research assistants (RAs) from DMNS conducted the data collection. The research assistants intercepted every third visitor at each site to produce a random sampling of visitors. As the study calls for a visitor's entry motivation, the RAs approached incoming adult patrons and asked them: "Can you help the museum learn a little bit more about why you came today?" RAs then handed the stack of 20 cards to the visitor, asked the visitor to take a moment to read through the cards and then to select the one card that best matched his or her personal reason for visiting that museum that day. In a majority of cases, visitors chose one card that reflected their motivation; however, in a few instances, they chose two to three top choices. In that scenario, the RA prompted the participant with a simple question: "I see you have chosen more than one card; if you look through those top cards again, can you pick out just one that best represents why you chose to come today?" Many people could choose one top card and the card number (each card was assigned a number 1 through 20 that was written on the back of the card) was recorded. Some patrons did not identify one motivation and in that case the RA recorded both numbers; however, those cases were removed during the analysis phase.

The Results

The table below provides a summary view of the dominant visitor motivation type for each institution. Each institution did have respondents that fell into each category as well as percentages for each category; however, what this chart provides is a quick look at the dominant visitor motivation type across institutions.

Rechargers view the Denver Botanic Gardens as a special place to "get-away" from the everyday crunch of life. People visit the Denver Art Museum and the Molly Brown House Museum to explore the buildings and collections. As explorers, they have a generic interest in art and history and are hoping to find something exciting and new; something that will capture their interests and as such, do not necessarily have a specific agenda. When visiting the remainder of the institutions — Buffalo Bill Museum and Grave, Butterfly Pavilion, Children's Museum of Denver, DMNS, Denver Zoo, Wildlife Experience — patrons identify as facilitators — they focus primarily on enabling the experience and learning of others in their accompanying social groups.

What does it mean to know what identities visitors seek to satisfy? As Falk argues, if museums do not satisfy a patron's need to recharge, facilitate, or explore, then they have not satisfied the patron as a museum visitor. However, beyond even satisfaction, how does knowing why visitors walk through the front door affect a museum's operations, programs, thoughts, and ideas? If the majority of a museum's visitors identify as explorers, how does that affect institu-

	Explorers	Facilitators	Experience Seekers	Professional/ Hobbyists	Rechargers
BB					
BP					
CM					
DAM					
DBG					
DMNS					
DZ					
MB					
WE					

Key: BB (Buffalo Bill Museum and Grave), BP (Butterfly Pavilion), CM (Children's Museum of Denver), DAM (Denver Art Museum), DBG (Denver Botanic Gardens), DMNS (Denver Museum of Nature & Science), DZ (Denver Zoo), MB (Molly Brown House Museum), WE (Wildlife Experience)

tional marketing plans? How can a development department capitalize on the knowledge that many of its museum's visitors see themselves as professional/hobbyists? Can an exhibition department use the knowledge that its core audience identifies as facilitators? When curators write labels, what might the graphics look like when trying to engage both experience seekers and professional/hobbyists? If the majority of a museum's guests consider themselves rechargers, how can visitor programmers use that information to inform their work? These are just a few questions to begin institutional conversations. None of this is to say that each institution should strive for targeting and reaching an equal balance of motivation types (unless that meets a museum's mission), or that one motivation is inherently "better" than another. Rather, what this instrument provides is additional information about museum visitors, of which every institution can use the data to make stronger, more strategic decisions.

Practical Applications: Denver Zoo

Denver Zoo, located just miles east of downtown, is Colorado's largest attended cultural organization, serving 1.97 million people in 2010 with on-grounds and outreach programs and experiences. The zoo collects limited demographic data on a regular basis (e.g., zip code data from ticket purchases, federal free and reduced lunch school statistics), and gathers intermittent demographics in visitor surveys. However, after participating in the citywide study on visitor motivation, it became clear to staff members that understanding visitor motivation identities may be just as useful, if not more, than demographic data when considering education, membership, marketing, and staff professional development. While demographic data provide Denver Zoo the ages, genders, ethnicities, and household incomes of its visitors, it does not provide the zoo with the "so what" answers that are needed when making choices in program development and delivery. After participating in, and receiving the results from, the citywide study in August 2010, Denver Zoo posed two essential research and evaluation questions: What motivates people to visit Denver Zoo, and are those motivations different at separate times of the year, and how can we maximize the quality of the visitor experience once we have a better understanding of our audience?

After receiving Denver Zoo's portion of the data from DMNS, staff was intrigued with the results and their implications for visitor experience programming. However, rather than rely on two days worth of data to make assumptions of the Zoo's visitors, Denver Zoo explored the idea of expanding the study to other days, including its free days. Denver Zoo is one of four Scientific and Cultural Facilities District organizations in Denver that offers free admission on certain days of the year. Denver Zoo has observed different demographics on free days compared to non-free days, and has seen less member visitation, more visitors from non-dominant cultural groups, and a greater number of patrons whose primary language is not English. A question arose: knowing that the demographics of Zoo visitors are different on free days compared to non-free days, is visitor motivation identity different amongst free days as well?

Along with free days, three additional "event types" were added to the research study. Staff wanted to know if little "i" identities varied by seasons, days-of-the-week, and/or event types. In the end, Denver Zoo, along with the original study funded by DMNS, collected visitor motivation identity data from 535 visitors on eight separate days that spanned 11 months: two late summer days (August 2010, n=107), two free days (January and February 2011, n=153), Sunday mornings (April and May 2011, n=117), and summer tourist season days (July 2011, n=158). The results of this study had profound implications, as the results have changed how Denver Zoo engages with its visitors and its non-visitors.

Researchers collected demographics of the 535 participants on gender, age, and Denver Zoo membership. Of those that participated in the study, 60% were female. The dominate age range was between 30 and 39 years old (43%, n=232), while the least dominate age range was over 70 years old (1%, n=4). Membership mean for three of the event types was 24% (membership data were not collected during the citywide study in order to replicate Falk's data collection instrument).

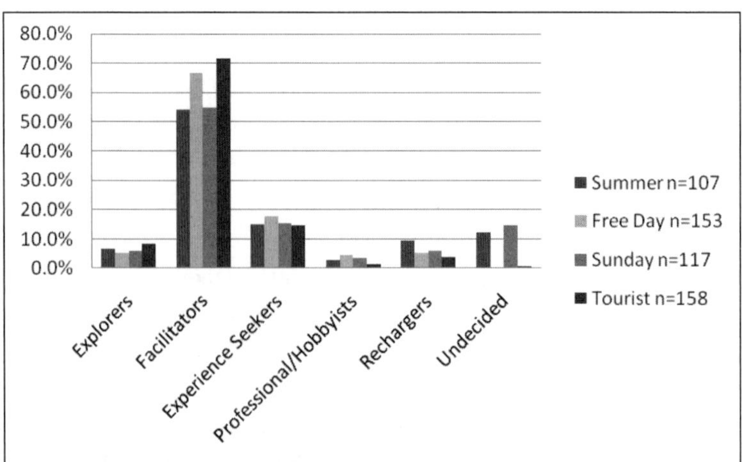

Visitor Identity-Related Motivations at Denver Zoo: These data were collected on eight days between August 2010 and July 2012. Each "event type" had two days of studies.

Member data varied among the event types at the zoo in which they were collected; for example, free day membership was 10%, Sunday morning membership was 45%, and summer tourist membership was 39%. According to zoo records, 35% of adult visitors were members on the two days data were collected by DMNS researchers in 2010.

Denver Zoo Visitors: Socially Motivated Guests

Across the eight days, member and non-member visitors identified themselves as facilitators, with 63% of the cards selected falling within this typology category. Visitors most frequently selected the card that read, “This is a good way for my family/friends to share quality time” (42% of the cards selected on all eight days). Falk would call these visitors “facilitating socializers.” There was variance in this particular card selection among the four event types. For example, during the late summer 2010 days study, 22% (n=24) of visitors surveyed selected the “quality time” card, however this number nearly tripled to 63% (n=99) during the tourist season days. The next most frequently selected card on the eight days of the study was from the facilitator typology as well — “I like to support the learning of

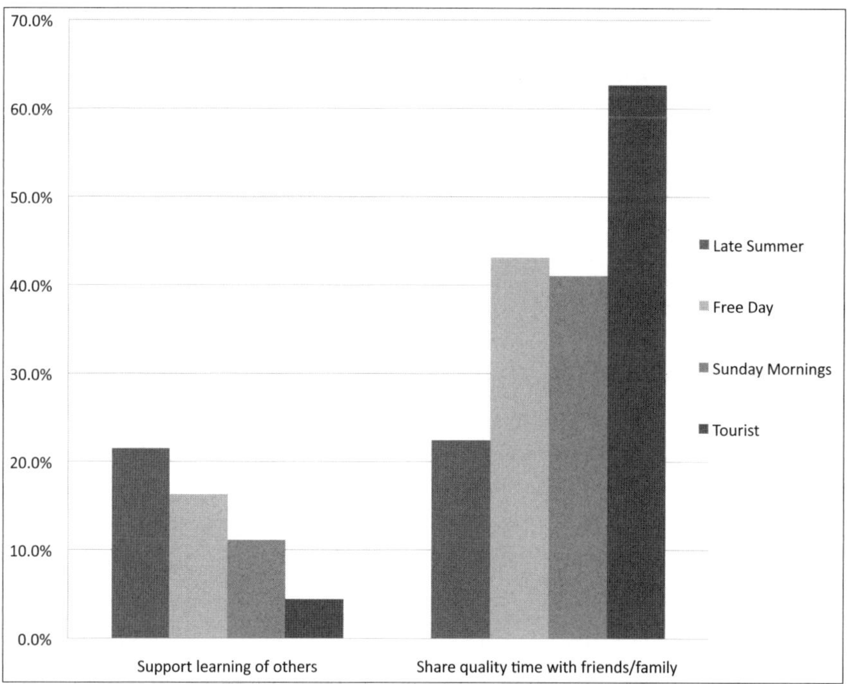

my children/significant other" was selected 13% of the time. Falk would call these visitors "facilitating parents" (Falk, 2009). However, tourist season visitors rarely selected this card (selection rate of 4%, n=7), compared to late summer days visitors (22%, n=23) and even free day visitors (16%, n=25). Ten percent more males (53% compared to 43% females) selected the card "This is a good way for my family/friends to share quality time," while the difference between genders selecting the card "I like to support the learning of my children/significant other" was minimal (12% male compared to 16% female). Members chose the card about spending more quality time with friends and family more often than non-members (61% and 48% respectively). While very few participants picked this card, nonmembers were more likely than members to pick the facilitator card "My family/friends learn things here they can't in other places" (4% compared to 1% of members).

Utilizing the Data to Better Understand Denver Zoo Visitors

Implications from the results have sparked conversations in many departments in Denver Zoo, as the data have provided a useful new lens for understanding Denver Zoo visitors. After analyzing the data, themes have emerged about Denver Zoo visitors:

Free day visitors may appear different from non-free day visitors, but their motivation for visiting is the same. Demographic data on Denver Zoo free day visitors are limited; however, front-line educators and other staff who work on-grounds during these events observe a more diverse audience than on non-free days. This diversity leads to a multitude of languages spoken on free days contributing to staff hesitation to enhance the visitor experience on these days. Yet, despite how free day visitors appear and behave the data indicate that they come to the Zoo for the same reasons as those who visit the Zoo on non-free days — to spend quality time with friends and family and to support the learning of those with whom they visit.

Summer tourist visitors visit Denver Zoo to spend quality time with friends and family. While the citywide data demonstrated an equal motivation to visit the Zoo for "quality time with friends and family" and "to support the learning of others" in late August 2010, the mid-July 2011 visitors presented drastically different motivations. Summer tourists selected "quality time" card 63% of the time, but the "learning of others" card only 4% of the time. The summer tourist event had the highest selection of the "quality time" card of the four events, surpassing the next closest event, which was 43% on free days.

Adult visitors are not necessarily motivated to visit Denver Zoo to learn for themselves. This confirms anecdotal data passed around by Zoo staff. The Zoo struggles with how to better understand why adults are not motivated to visit Denver Zoo for their own learning.

Changes at Denver Zoo

In order to address the question, "How can Denver Zoo maximize the quality of the visitor experience once it has a better understanding of its audience?" the following programs and ideas have developed as a result of this study:

Staff training on visitor motivation identity: Denver Zoo's Visitor Experience Team (VE Team) began working to create a customer interaction training to enhance the communication skills of zoo staff. The training aimed to provide tools that would allow staff members to more easily engage visitors in meaningful conversations. As part of this training, the VE Team reviewed the final report for *Why Zoos and Aquariums Matter* (WZAM), published by Falk et al in 2009, in which he outlines visitor motivation.[12] The VE Team believed the Falk identity model offered a practical tool for staff professional development — and now they had specific data about where their own visitors fit into the model. The Team identified two goals for the training class: 1) to give staff effective tools with which to engage visitors, and 2) to move staff beyond demographics (capital "I" identities) and towards identity related motivations (little "i" identities).

Fifty-five staff members, representing 80% of the zoo's departments, attended one of two hour-and-a-half long interactive trainings. Presenters briefly described the WZAM study and detailed each of the five motivation types. They displayed the WZAM study results, the citywide results from Denver study, and then compared Denver Zoo's results with the other participating cultural institutions. Presenting the citywide numbers gave many staff a concrete look at what was, up until that point, an abstract, academic concept that existed only in journals. Now, staff could begin to envision how they could practically apply the notion of identities to their institution and programs. Next, presenters asked staff to identify which current programs were satisfying which motivation types and to consider which motivation types were not targeted by any programming. To make it "real" for zoo staff, presenters asked the participants to brainstorm what observations and/or questions they could use in conversations with visitors to ascertain a visitor's motivation type and to recommend an appropriate program or exhibition at the zoo that would satisfy that motivation type.

The training met desired goals and outcomes. All staff who participated indicated they discovered new ways to interact with different types of visitors.

Many indicated they will now consider visitor motivation types when designing a program. The selected staff who participated requested additional training for the entire Zoo staff and all volunteers. Requests have been made to offer the training again for staff and to extend the offering to volunteers. Further, staff members now utilize a common language about visitors based on the motivation types, better enabling communication of guest needs and wants.

Revised marketing strategies targeting facilitators: The Marketing and Communications Department is considering how to use the data in developing strategic marketing campaigns. Denver Zoo's current marketing slogan, "Every time you visit helps animals," was recently tested with patrons. Although staff loves the mission and conservation-centric slogan, it did not resonate with or motivate people to visit. Coupled with the results of the visitor motivation identity study, Marketing and Communications will explore a campaign that focuses on attracting audiences who are seeking fun, quality, and educational experiences with family and friends.

Free day staff training and revised programming: Education and Volunteer Services staff members deliver education programming at stations set-up throughout the zoo on free days during the year. Feedback from staff indicates that free day visitors do not engage in learning like non-free day visitors; thereby making it challenging for staff to accomplish their programmatic goals. Zoo educators received special training in Fall 2011 using identity-motivation types as a framework from which to begin brainstorming new programming and methods for engaging with free day visitors. Additionally, an outcome of the training was to increase positive staff attitudes about free day visitors.

New mobile phone application based on motivation identities: The zoo is exploring visitor motivation types to create better and more appropriate downloadable tours for Denver Zoo's phone application launched in late 2011. After the launch, Visitor Services staff will evaluate the application with an eye towards trying to see if a correlation exists between visitor motivation types and downloads.

What Does it All Mean?

In several cases, the results of this study spawned just as many questions as answers. Each institution grappled with the overall, citywide results as well as its individual results. Each had to think about what it meant to have certain typologies rise to the top and others fall to the bottom. In some cases, it challenged an institution's view of its visitorship; in other cases it confirmed anecdotal ideas of patrons. In each case; however, regardless of which typology rose to the top, the instrument and the data worked — in that it created conversations, follow-up, and implementation of more tailored and needs-based programs geared towards engaging visitors. In addition, the typology provided a common vocabulary from which practitioners from a wide range of cultural institutions could now converse. The Falk Visitor Identity-Related Motivation Typology provides a snap-shot of who museum visitors are now, allowing institutions to make stronger, more strategic decisions.

Notes

1. Falk, J. H. *Identity and Museum Visitor Experience*. Walnut Creek, CA: Left Coast Press, 2009.
2. Kelly, J.R. "Situational and Social Factors in Leisure Decisions." Technical Report, 1977. ERIC #:ED153143.
3. Beard, J.G. & Mounir, R. "Measuring leisure satisfaction." *Journal of Leisure Research*, 12 (1980): 20–33.
4. Manfredo, M.J. & Driver, B.L. "Measuring leisure motivation: A meta-analysis of the recreation experience preference scales." *Journal of Leisure Research*, 28, no. 3 (1996): 188–213. Hood, M. "Leisure Criteria of Family Participation and Non-Participation in Museums." Technical Report. Columbus, OH: Hood Associates, 1981. Moussouri, T. *Family agendas and family learning in hands-on museums*. Unpublished doctoral dissertations. University of Leicester, Leicester, England, 1997. Packer, J. & Ballentyne, R. (2002). "Motivational factors and the visitor experience: A comparison of three sites." *Curator*, 45 (2002): 183–173. Yalowitz, S.S. "Personality and motivation in visitor satisfaction." *Visitor Studies Today*, 5, no.1 (2002): 14–17.
5. Falk, J.H. "A Multi-Factor Investigation of Variables Affecting Informal Science Learning." *Final Report to the National Science Foundation*. Annapolis, MD: Institute for Learning Innovation, 2004.
6. Falk, 2009.
7. Ibid.
8. Recently, Falk has added two motivational types: *Respectful Pilgrims* visit out of a sense of duty or obligation to honor the memory of those represented by an institution/memorial and *Affinity Seekers* are motivated to visit because a particular museum or more likely exhibition speaks to the visitor's sense of heritage and/or personhood. Falk, John. "Contextualizing Falk's Visitor Identity-Related Motivation Model." *Visitor Studies Today*. In press.
9. Ballantyne, Roy. *Review of Identity and the Museum Visitor Experience*. Left Coast Press, Inc. (2010), http://www.lcoastpress.com/book.php?id=214 (accessed June 2011).
10. Bickford, A. "Review of *Identity and the Museum Visitor Experience*." *Curator*, 53(2): 247–255.
11. The words of John Falk's instrument©, five categories, four cards per category: *Explorers:* I went because it satisfies my curiosity; I am not an expert but I like to learn about things; The museum is more inspiring than going to the mall or a movie; These are the kinds of places people like me go. *Facilitators:* My friends/family learn things here they can't other places; My wife/partner/husband made me come; I like to support the learning of my children/significant others; This is a good way for my family/friends to share quality time. *Professional/hobbyists:* I was hoping to find out more about something in particular; This is my hobby and I come all the time; It relates to the kind of work I do and I find it useful; I'm quite knowledgeable but like to keep up with what's new. *Experience Seekers:* I was told that

it is one of the best places to visit around here; This place is a landmark in this community; I wanted to be able to say that I'd been there; I wanted to have fun. *Rechargers:* I feel at peace in these surroundings; I find going helps me get away from the normal rush of life; I discover things about myself when I come here; I don't get to be in spaces like this every day.

12. Falk, J.H.; Reinhard, E.M.; Vernon, C.L.; Bronnenkant, K.; Deans, N.L.; Heimlich, J.E. *Why Zoos & Aquariums Matter: Assessing the Impact of a Visit.* Silver Spring, MD: Association of Zoos & Aquariums, 2007.

About the Authors

Laureen Trainer is currently the Manager of Visitor Research & Program Evaluation at the Denver Museum of Nature & Science. She worked in the museum education field for eight years before returning to school for her Masters in Museum Studies from the University of Colorado, Boulder.

Marley Steele-Inama is the Manager of Education Research and Evaluation at Denver Zoo. Ms. Steele-Inama has 13 years experience developing, delivering, managing, and evaluating zoo education programming. Ms. Steele-Inama received an MAEd in Curriculum and Instruction from the University of Denver.

Amber Christopher is the Vice President of Guest Services and New Business at Denver Zoo. In this position Ms. Christopher manages several operational areas including Admissions, Guest Relations and Security. She has a BSBA in Hotel, Restaurant and Tourism and an MCIS from the University of Denver.

Bringing Art to Life through Multi-Sensory Tours

Wendy L. Dodek

Abstract Learning occurs in myriad ways yet most art museums remain wedded to visual instruction. Adult visitors touring the galleries are offered audio guides or lecture style tours to complement the visual but are there other ways to enhance learning? This article reports on a case study that found that active, multi-sensory experiences in art museums can encourage adults to construct meaning and more fully engage with art.

Multi-sensory experiences have become the norm in children's and science museums and are lauded for enhancing enjoyment and increasing learning opportunities for young visitors. How might adults benefit from such offerings, in particular in art museums, where aesthetic appreciation is highly valued?

Touching objects opens up entirely new ways to experience art: through texture, weight, volume, and temperature. Auditory and olfactory connections to art are also beginning to be explored, prompted by civil rights legislation mandating accessibility for all visitors regardless of their abilities. Staff must think creatively and develop special tours that cater to multiple senses. But why are we creating these multi-sensory experiences for a narrow band of visitors when they have the potential to benefit all visitors regardless of their visual acuity or other physical limitations?

Research suggests multi-sensory experiences could benefit a significant percentage of the population who are not visual learners and prefer other sensory modalities to make meaning in the world. Studies date back to the 1930s when art educator Viktor Lowenfeld conducted a series of experiments and concluded

Journal of Museum Education, Volume 37, Number 1, Spring 2012, pp. 115–124.

that people fit into one of two categories: visual learners or "haptical" learners — those who need stimulus from touch or kinesthetics to effectively function in the world. And while almost half of his research subjects were visual learners, another one-quarter of the sample was identified as haptical learners with the remaining individuals exhibiting no clear tendencies toward either mode of learning.[1]

Numerous other researchers followed including psychologist Howard Gardner, probably most widely recognized for his expansive view of learning. He advanced the theory that humans are capable of multiple intelligences, not just conventionally accepted logical and linguistic abilities as measured in standardized tests. He argues people naturally learn based on a combination of the particular "intelligences" they favor.[2] Less conventional learning methods have also been explored by educators including literacy expert Lawrence Baines who noted students who engage with multiple senses "interact more intensely" and "retain what they've learned for longer periods of time."[3]

While such general scholarship on learning exists, research has not focused specifically on outcomes of sensory experiences within art museums, especially for adults. There are indicators of the positive value of this type of experience, however, from several recent studies that could shed light on multi-sensory applications for museums. In one long-term study, conducted by noted education and evaluation experts John H. Falk and Lynn D. Dierking, of over 2000 visitors it was the sensory experiences in the museum: the smells, light, even the sensation of the rug that was retained in the subconscious and became trigger points of memory.[4] Another study launched in 1998 of 116 geographically diverse museums investigated attributes of successful learning programs for adult visitors. Among the relevant findings was a desire among adults for active, interesting programs rather than passive lectures. A full 70 percent of respondents rated "active, hands-on activities" as "very important" to their learning and enjoyment, higher than "interacting with other participants" or having a "comfortable physical setting." The authors concluded, "Sights, smells, and sounds combine to create memorable experiences that may have a lasting and possibly transformative effect on the participants."[5]

The studies described above suggest that visitors drawn into an experience through their senses make deeper connections leading to the possibility that greater learning could ensue. Working with that hypothesis, a small multi-sensory interpretive program was developed and tested with visitors. This article reports on its findings and considers possible benefits for art museums.

Methods

This case study explored adult visitors' reactions to multi-sensory art museum tours. Questions guiding the study included: what types of learning could be expected from multi-sensory tours compared to standard tours; which sensory stimuli are effective in engaging visitors and what types of galleries should be contenders for these types of tours? The study was conducted at the Museum of Fine Arts, Boston as part of the "Spotlight Talks" program in 2009 and 2010. Spotlight talks are short gallery tours, just 15 minutes in length, and focus on one to two objects. Selection of artwork was a major consideration. Learning approaches might be different based on the type of artwork chosen: paintings versus sculptures, for example, or Western art versus non-Western art.

For this case study, it was possible to test two different types of art in two different themed galleries. Half of the tours were conducted in a gallery of African sculptural art, presumably unfamiliar to most of the museum's visitors and the other half in a European Impressionist paintings gallery with widely known artists. While not attempting to represent the universe of art, it does present an opportunity to explore visitor reaction to two different types of art from different cultures. The four art objects presented in the talks are shown below.

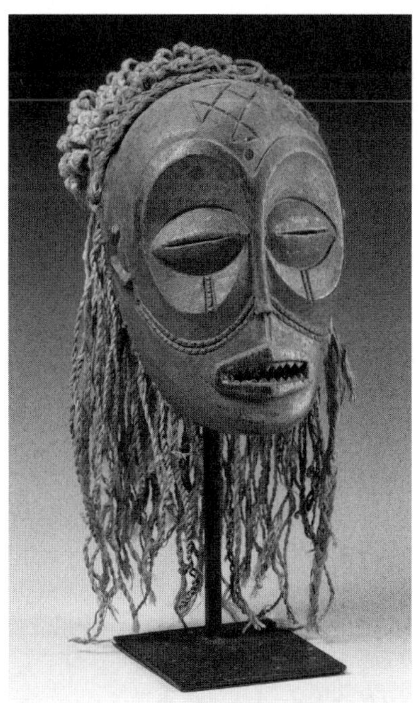

Mask (mwana pwo), Democratic Republic of the Congo (Chokwe, 19th to early 20th century). Wood, fiber, metal, and pigment, 19.05 cm. (7 ½ in.), Gift of William E. and Bertha L. Teel, 1996. 379. Photograph © Museum of Fine Arts, Boston

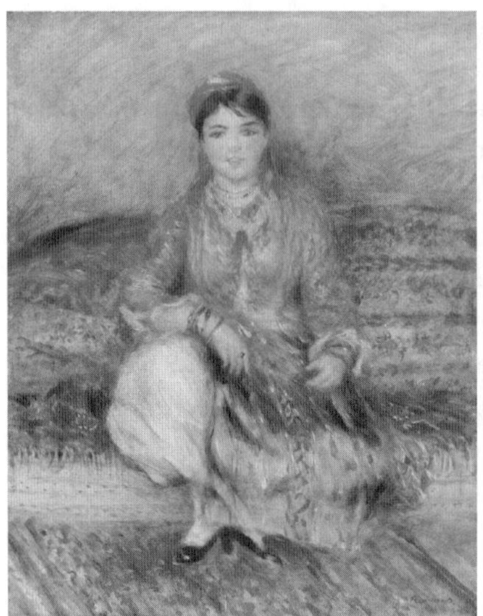

Pierre-Auguste Renoir, Algerian Girl, 1881, Oil on canvas, 50.8 x 40.6 cm (20 x 16 in.), Juliana Cheney Edwards collection, 39.677. Photograph © Museum of Fine Arts, Boston

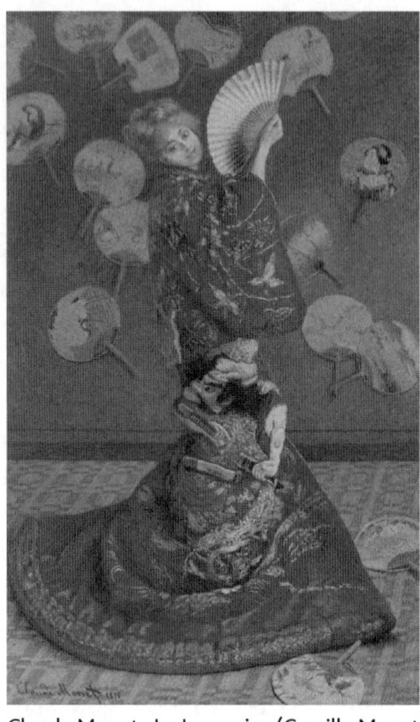

Claude Monet, La Japonaise (Camille Monet in Japanese Costume), 1876, Oil on canvas, 231.8 x 142.3 cm (91 ¼ x 56 in.), 1951 Purchase Fund, 56.147 . Photograph © Museum of Fine Arts, Boston

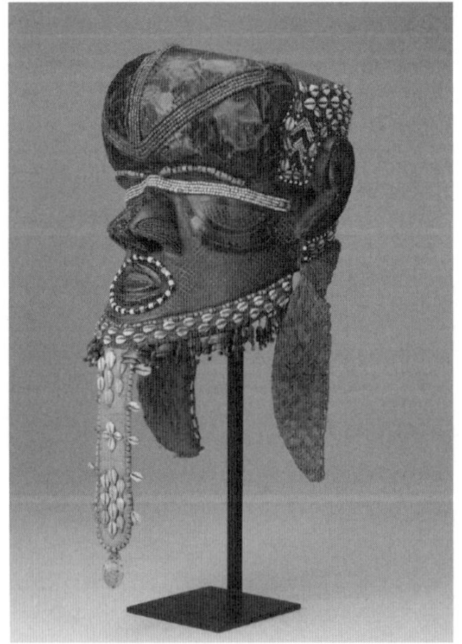

Mask (bwoom), Democratic Republic of Congo (Kuba, 20th century). Wood, copper, beads, cloth, shells, and seeds, 33.02 cm. (13 in.). Gift of William E. And Bertha L. Teel, 1994. 414. Photograph © Museum of Fine Arts, Boston

Half of the tours offered were conventional "standard" tours — an exclusively verbal presentation of information and the other half "multi-sensory" tours, whereby relevant objects that appeal to the sense of touch, smell, and hearing were included. For the African talks: visitors smelled and held a smoky Chokwe tourist mask similar to the one on display, listened to traditional music, held a Royal Kuba necklace, and were given the gift of an African cowrie shell, similar to the decoration on one of the masks.[6] For the European talks, the following objects were selected: an *uchikake* (type of Japanese kimono) similar to the one depicted in the Monet painting, a collection of traditional Algerian spices intended to simulate the aroma Renoir might have experienced when painting in Algeria, and lastly, traditional Algerian folk music known as *Rai*, music that dates back to the time Renoir was painting in Algeria.[7]

A survey instrument was developed to test whether the addition of sensory objects stimulated the formation of memories that would ultimately increase visitor knowledge. Two weeks after the tours, participants were contacted by phone and interviewed for approximately 10 to 15 minutes.[8]

Findings

A total of 252 visitors attended the 24 spotlight talks and 80 visitors — 20 from each type of tour — participated in the interviews. Visitors were very enthusiastic about the inclusion of multi-sensory objects in the tours. Several individuals attending the European talks referenced the weight of the kimono and how they learned it was heavier than they thought from looking at the painting. "Fun to let people try it on and feel the fabric. You feel like you really are participating in the artwork."

Visitors attending the African talks were more passionate about this type of learning. One participant described being transported to a different place and developing a new understanding of the artwork when smelling and feeling the smoky Chokwe mask. "Really cool that you could smell the smoky odor, takes you right to the place at that moment." Another participant said, "Holding and smelling the mask I had a vision of people around the fire, at night, ritual dancing... conjures up a scene." The value of the cowrie shells was more than simply the ability to hold a small object that could be found in Africa and seen on the mask. Visitors were happy to have a souvenir of their experience as the following comments illustrate: "I put them in a dish and so every time I see them in the living room, I think about the mask." "Something in the handing out of the shells that added weight, that made it real, just having something to hold was a tactile link to Africa."

Visitors were clearly enthusiastic about the multi-sensory experience but could this enthusiasm translate into learning? In an attempt to determine if multi-sensory talks would make a more lasting impact participants were asked to identify the most memorable artwork from their visit to the museum. Results showed that the multi-sensory participants were significantly more likely to mention one of the art objects included in the tour than those who attended the conventional tours. The distinction was more pronounced among those attending the African talks where just one-quarter of the standard tour participants named one of the two objects in the talk as most memorable from their visit at the MFA. This compares to over two-thirds of the visitors who attended the African multi-sensory talk. More multi-sensory European tour participants (compared to the control group) mentioned one of the paintings but the differential was not as great, as indicated in Graph 1.

How likely are these visitors to add the information from the talk to their reservoir of knowledge and perhaps build a long-term memory for the future? One approach to exploring this question is to look at post-tour connections: if visitors shared the experience with others, read more about the artwork, or returned to look at the artwork. All of these activities would help cement the experience in their memories. Since the survey was conducted just two weeks after the tour, results can only hint at the development of long-term learning.

The most basic connection would be communicating some of the content of the talks to friends and family. The findings in Graph 2 show visitors attending the multi-sensory tours were significantly more likely to have answered that they shared their experience with loved ones. The difference again is more pronounced among those who attended the African talks.

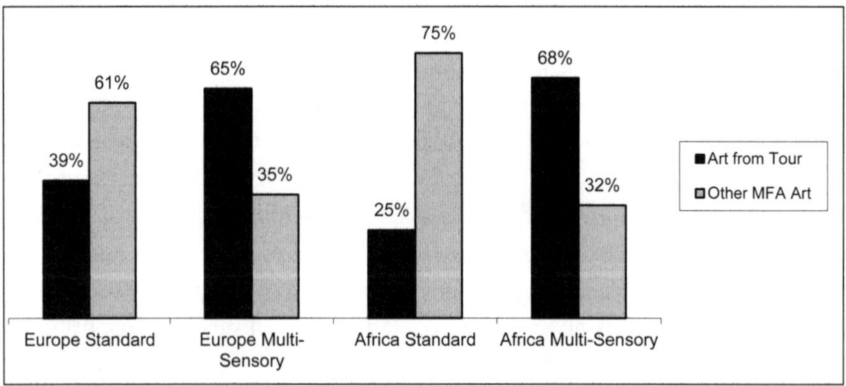

Graph 1: Artwork Most Remembered from Visit

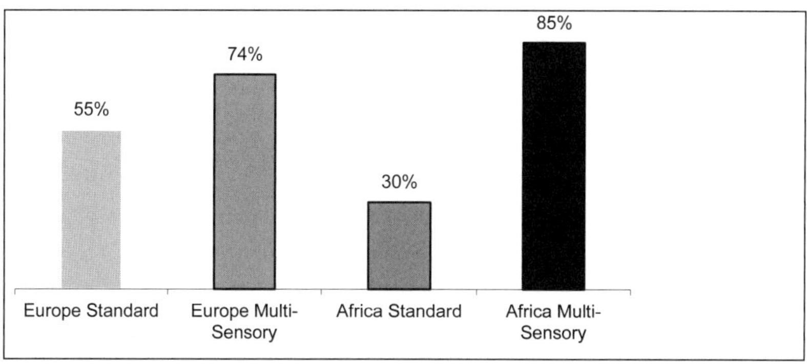

Graph 2: Shared with Others?

Visitors were asked during the phone interview to provide details they recalled from the talks. Certainly a better recitation of information is not sufficient to project future learning. Some individuals are much more gifted at recall. Younger visitors presumably retain information longer. Participants attending both types of talks had factual errors in the recall. The most universal finding, regardless of type of artwork experienced or type of tour attended was the ability to recall concrete details, especially if surprising or counterintuitive. Following the European talks, visitors recalled several details of the painting, "La Japanaise." They mentioned Monet's wife wearing a blonde wig, the warrior painted on the kimono, the startled look on the Japanese woman in a fan. In the African galleries, visitors recalled the pointy teeth on one mask being a sign of beauty, the male dancer wearing false breasts and a padded fanny to represent the female spirit.

Even though concrete details were recalled by participants in both types of tours, there were differences. Those attending the multi-sensory talks recalled more details and extrapolated those details more frequently to their own lives. The tangible objects helped reinforce the museum experience. For example, 14 multi-sensory tour visitors recalled how the sea shells were once used for currency compared to just three visitors from the standard tours. Those who held a shell and took it home described how they explained the meaning of the shell to their families. One woman gave the shell to her son who collects shells but was excited that this one represented money in another culture. Respondents from both types of European talks commented on the kimono but only those who attended the multi-sensory talk and personally held the kimono offered more detailed comments referencing the "thickness and lusciousness" of it. Perhaps this is the most important value of multi-sensory learning gleaned from this case study: visitors are able to retain more information from their experience and then make greater connections to their personal lives.

Education theorists believe learning is an ongoing process with individuals actively exploring their own interests to build upon their own knowledge base of understanding.[9] Therefore, to encourage visitors to retain new information, museum educators need to do more than provide new information but also look for ways to create connections to visitors' reservoir of experiences. This multi-sensory approach to gallery tours could be one way of building such critical connections.

Selection of Objects

The selection of objects is an essential part of developing multi-sensory talks. Not all of the objects were equally well-received by visitors attending tours. Most importantly, objects need to be perceived as having a clear connection to the artwork. The kimono seemed to have walked out of the Monet painting. Engaging the sense of smell, such as the smoked Chokwe mask or the Algerian spices, surprised and pleased attendees. Giving visitors a souvenir, tangible proof of their experience, such as the cowrie shell, was not only appealing but offers the promise of long-term memory reinforcement. The music, on the other hand, provided more passive involvement and was not rated as highly.

Overall, the addition of sensory objects was credited with helping build retention, creating a positive atmosphere, and giving context to the artwork. There were differences in visitor attitudes based on artwork and culture. Visitors attending the African tours were more enthusiastic about the inclusion of related objects in the talks and several insisted this should become the new standard approach for museum tours. "When you go through African galleries you really want to touch: the rough woods, the barks, grasses... I always wanted to touch these things." Another participant added, "It reminds us this is not a painting and shouldn't be isolated from human contact." Some visitors attending the European gallery talks described inclusion of multi-sensory objects in Western galleries of painting as icing on the cake, a nice addition, but not essential.

Conclusions

The results point to visitors attending talks incorporating multi-sensory objects developing stronger initial memories and making greater connections from the artwork to their personal lives than the control group. While this case study focused on the educational value of multi-sensory learning for adults, there are other reasons museums may consider adopting this type of tour experience.

Multi-sensory tours can transform museums from intimidating places where touch is forbidden to more accessible, friendly environments. This approach also offers an opportunity to create tours that would be compelling to a larger segment of the museum audience. Individuals with children would find these tours more engaging for the entire family. Multi-sensory tours also open up new possibilities for seniors, a growing segment of the population, some with visual or audio limitations but who do not want to be segregated into special tours. Even for mainstream adults, multi-sensory tours help mitigate visual overload by providing additional ways to experience art, to complement the visual and alleviate museum fatigue.

It should be stressed multi-sensory learning is not intended to minimize the visual experience. Visitors will always revel in the visual splendor of the artwork. Engaging visitors with all of their senses, not exclusively sight, encourages them to slow down and spend more time thinking and reflecting on the significance of the artwork, as well as appreciating the aesthetics.

Research Limitations

The results of this study raise intriguing possibilities of connecting adult visitors to artwork in lasting ways. A few limitations regarding the size and scope of this study should be noted. Starting with sample size, while 252 visitors attended the 24 spotlight talks in the European and African galleries, only 80 were interviewed. There was no attempt to gather a representative sample; all visitors who agreed to participate in the survey were interviewed. Therefore, it is not known whether it is possible to extrapolate all of the findings to the larger population of art museum goers.

Another limiting factor was the short amount of time, just weeks, between the spotlight talk and the interview date. While the findings clearly show more short-term memories have been forged through this gallery learning approach; it would take an additional survey, conducted over several months, to determine if the respondents continue to interweave the new information gained to create long-term memories. The results of the survey give a strong indication that would be the case. As one visitor said very simply, when explaining why she liked the multi-sensory style tour, "Brilliant: it brings art to life."

Notes

1. Viktor Lowenfeld, "Tests for Visual and Haptical Aptitudes." *American Journal of Psychology* 58.1 (1945): 110–111.

2. Howard Gardner, *Intelligence Reframed: Multiple Intelligences for the 21st Century* (New York: Basic Books, 1999), 41.
3. Lawrence Baines, *A Teacher's Guide to Multisensory Learning: Improving Literacy by Engaging the Senses* (Alexandria, Virginia: Association for Supervision and Curriculum Development, 2008), x.
4. John H. Falk and Lynn D. Dierking. *The Museum Experience* (Washington: Whalesback Books, 1992), 100.
5. Bonnie Sachatello-Sawyer, et al., *Adult Museum Programs: Designing Meaningful Experiences* (Walnut Creek, CA: Alta Mira Press, 2002), 117, 120.
6. The Chokwe mask was borrowed from the MFA Teel Curator of African and Oceanic Art, Christraud Geary. The music was borrowed from the Loeb Music Library at Harvard University. The royal Kuba necklace was borrowed from the African specialist and curator at the Peabody Museum of Archaeology and Ethnology, Harvard University, Monni Adams. The African cowrie shells were purchased at a local bead store.
7. The *uchikake* was acquired in Japan and belongs to the author. Algerian spices were purchased at local spice shops. The music was borrowed from the Loeb Music Library at Harvard University.
8. Visitors were told the author was working on a thesis on gallery learning methods. They were not told the topic was specifically about multi-sensory learning to avoid any bias in their responses.
9. Knud Illeris, *How We Learn: Learning and Non-Learning in School and Beyond* (New York: Routledge Press, 1997), 28. Nina Jensen, "Children, Teenagers, and Adults in a Museum: A Developmental Perspective." (*Museum News* 61.3 1982): 268–274.

About the Author

Wendy Dodek is an Adjunct Educator at the Museum of Fine Arts, Boston. This case study formed the basis of her thesis, "Sensing Art: Creating Lasting, Lively, Learning Experiences for Adults," and won the Dean's Prize for outstanding thesis in 2010 at Harvard University Extension School. She continues to offer monthly spotlight talks at the MFA that incorporate sensory elements from aromatic sweet grass in the Native American basketry talk to cacao pods in the talk exploring chocolate from Mayan times to the Colonial era. Ms. Dodek is also Principal of Insight Research & Training with extensive background in qualitative research.

The Death and Life of the Great American School System

How Testing and Choice are Undermining Education

By Diane Ravitch

Reviewed by Lois A. Stoehr

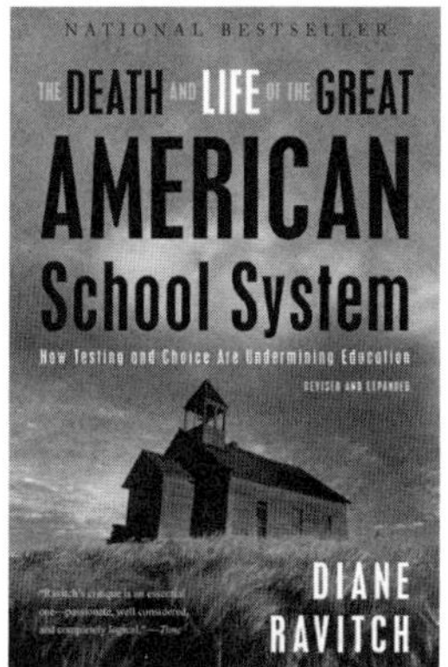

242 pages. Basic Books. 2010.
$33.95 (hardcover)
ISBN978–0–465–01491–0

In the spring of 2011, I had two experiences that cast me into a temporary state of despair. First, I attended a regular bi-monthly meeting of local museum educators where the entire discussion quickly devolved into a debate about the best way to distribute our school program brochures — as if that were the sole factor influencing our steadily decreasing attendance. The following week, a colleague from a nearby museum and I met with administrators from two local school districts to discuss ways that schools and museums could partner to better serve the students in our community. Our hope was that we could foster an understanding of museums as more than just purveyors of field trips, but as organizations with resources and expertise who are equally concerned about the education and well being of children.

The meeting began with the administrators' expression of incredulity that Winterthur school programs could even begin to address *one* of the state standards we address during every program, let alone do justice to *all* of them. This incredulity belied a stance that such standards were to be covered sequentially, discipline by discipline, and that museum programs were not worthwhile because they could not adequately replace an in-class lesson. The meeting ended with a tentative invitation for my colleague and me to spend a grand total of 15 minutes at a statewide meeting promoting our cause.

A few days later I happened to encounter an interview with author Diane Ravitch regarding standardized testing. While I had had a tendency to blame testing in the abstract for declining school program attendance at my museum, I had done so without fully understanding what testing or its implications actually were. Fresh off of the two experiences above, I was eager to see the bigger picture. Why are schools so reluctant to partner with museums, who ostensibly share the goal of instilling students with a love of learning? And how can museums be more sensitive to the needs of schools, whose metrics for measuring success are clearly *not* congruent with our own?

As it turned out, the interview pointed me toward Ravitch's book *The Death and Life of the Great American School System*, which had been released in 2010. The book merited particular attention because Ravitch originally supported approaches to reform movements that she now opposes. A historian of education, she served as Assistant Secretary of Education during the George H. W. Bush administration, while during the Clinton administration she served on the National Assessment Governing Board, which oversees the agency responsible for federal testing. I bought a copy, read it in three days, and recommended it to everyone in our local museum educators' group. I also recommended it to my staff of part-time school program guides, who have often pined for the days when Spring would bring an endless caravan of school buses to our front door and wondered why that seasonal phenomenon no longer occurs.

The Death and Life of the Great American School System provides, in a straightforward and jargon-free style, an excellent overview of the challenges currently facing public education in the U.S. These challenges directly affect each of the students who participate in museum programs, as well as their teachers and principals. Perhaps even more importantly, the same challenges also impact the students who *do not* participate in the many programs museums offer.

What are the challenges Ravitch identifies? She lists No Child Left Behind as the primary driving force in education, a law that demands 100% of American students achieve "proficiency" in reading and math by the year 2014. Each state determines what, exactly, "proficiency" means, which has led to a great range of standards — and often very low ones at that. Ravitch argues that, because the test scores in reading and math alone determine whether schools should be shuttered or reconfigured, or lauded and rewarded, testing and test preparation demand extraordinary proportions of class time, usually at the expense of a more nuanced education. Although I have certainly been aware of No Child Left Behind, these insights gave me a greater empathy for the teachers I had heretofore considered simply too uninspired to schedule field trips.

According to Ravitch, the bi-partisan support of "school choice," especially when the choice is a charter school, is the second major factor currently "undermining education," as the subtitle of the book states. An outgrowth of the more controversial voucher program, charter schools provide a publicly-funded alternative to regular public schools, often taking the most motivated students and faculty with them. Ravitch argues that charter schools were originally intended "not to compete with public schools, but to support them" through their role as "research and development laboratories for discovering better ways of educating hard-to-educate children." She concludes that charter schools are actually doing the opposite: competing for students and weakening the sense of community centered on neighborhood schools.[1] Furthermore, she states that, "There was little evidence that charter schools were generically better than public schools. Nothing in the record suggested that the entire sector was successful, that any charter school was better than *any* public school."[2]

As No Child Left Behind and school choice exemplify, museum educators are directly affected by education reform; hence, we would all be better served to be more aware of current trends. *Death and Life* is rounded-out by frank discussion regarding accountability, merit pay, teachers unions, the exertion of political might, and the unprecedented influence of philanthropic foundations on shaping the national education agenda. Ravitch also presents case studies for three different school districts that demonstrate how overzealous (and underinformed) leaders can quickly wreak havoc in their efforts to force adherence to a single pedagogical method; reorganize based on a strict, top-down corporate model; or exercise some combination of the two. Often these efforts are supported by outside individuals with extremely deep pockets, including Eli Broad and Walmart heir John Walton, who each gave generously in 2002 to the campaign funds of candidates for the San Diego school board.[3]

Because we work in a field that relies heavily on philanthropy, the role of major foundations in education reform, described in the chapter "The Billionaire Boys' Club," was especially eye-opening. With their combined resources, the Gates, Broad, and Walton foundations have come "to exercise vast influence in strategic investments in school reform," according to Ravitch.[4] She goes on to say that as the policy goals of these foundations "converged in the first decade of the twenty-first century," they "set the policy agenda not only for school districts, but also for states and even the U.S. Department of Education."[5] The lesson for readers, of course, is to try to prevent the tail from wagging the dog, which is achieved only through vigilant cognizance and involvement.

Involvement, along with a strong national curriculum in the humanities and sciences, well-educated teachers, and a re-examined use of testing, is a critical component of the "vision of education we want for our children and our society," argues Ravitch.[6] "Schools do not exist in isolation," she writes. "They are part of the larger society. Schooling requires the active participation of many, including students, families, public officials, local organizations, and the larger community."[7] It goes without saying that museum educators are, as both professionals and individuals, part of that larger community—and we cannot afford to be myopic. It is essential for us to understand the external forces and challenges facing public schools and evolve accordingly. Though we may pride ourselves on thinking about these issues at the national level, we should also be involved in the districts our museums serve, or at the very least, in the districts in which we live. Investigate the history of your local school districts, research the candidates for your local school board—and then vote. While no candidate will ever run solely on a pro-museum ticket, as proponents of broad educational experiences we should support that ideal however we can.

Finally, as a profession, it is no longer enough to merely concern ourselves with how we advertise our programs; we must give increasing weight to the message we want to deliver. We cannot assume that schools consider the hands-on and interdisciplinary programs we offer worthwhile; we must strive to demonstrate for parents, teachers, administrators—and anyone else who will listen—why those programs matter. Furthermore, whether we are primarily responsible for school, family, or adult programming, or even exhibition development and design, we should continue conveying to audiences of all ages the idea that learning can happen anywhere, at any time, and can even be *fun*. We must do our part to ensure that the No Child Left Behind generation is prepared to appreciate and support the rich cultural resources that the museums in their communities provide.

Notes

1. Ravitch, Diane. *The Death and Life of the Great American School System; How Testing and Choice are Undermining Education* (New York: Basic Books, 2010).
2. Ibid., 142.
3. Ibid., 55.
4. Ibid., 200.
5. Ibid., 200.
6. Ibid., 231.
7. Ibid., 239.

About the Reviewer

Lois A. Stoehr is Associate Curator of Education at Winterthur Museum, Garden & Library, where she oversees programming for school and family audiences. She is a graduate of the Winterthur Program in Early American Culture, was the curator of the 2007 exhibition K is for Kids, and has spoken at conferences in Virginia, Texas, and the U.K

LEFT COAST PRESS, INC.
1630 N MAIN STREET #400
WALNUT CREEK CA 94596

PRSRT STD
U S POSTAGE
P A I D
ANN ARBOR MI
PERMIT 87

*********************AUTO**MIXED ADC 150
CAROLINE GOESER
2570 EUCLID HEIGHTS BLVD
CLEVELAND HEIGHTS OH 44106-2726